9/01

GRAVEYARDS OF CHICAGO

The People, History, Art, and Lore of Cook County Cemeteries

D0168794

Matt Hucke
Ursula Bielski

First Edition

Lake Claremont Press

P.O. Box 25291
Chicago, Illinois 60625
www.lakeclaremont.com

Graveyards of Chicago:
The People, History, Art, and Lore of Cook County Cemeteries

Published November 1999 by:

Lake Claremont Press
4650 N. Rockwell St.
Chicago, IL 60625
773/583-7800
www.lakeclaremont.com

Copyright © 1999 by Ursula Bielski and Matt Hucke
All photographs copyright © 1996-1999 by Matt Hucke
First Edition

Publisher's Cataloging-in-Publication
(Provided by Quality Books, Inc.)

Hucke, Matt.
   Graveyards of Chicago : the people, history,
art, and lore of Cook County cemeteries / Matt
Hucke, Ursula Bielski. — 1st ed.
   p. cm.
   Includes bibliographical references and index.
   LCCN: 99-62509
   ISBN: 0-9642426-4-8

   1. Cemeteries—Illinois—Cook County—
Guidebooks. 2. Sepulchral monuments—Illinois—
Cook County. 3. Cook county (Ill.)—Guidebooks.
I. Bielski, Ursula. II. Title.

F547.C7H83 1999   929'.50977731
                             QBI99-1513

**Printed in the United States of America by United Graphics,
an employee-owned company in Mattoon, Illinois.**

05 04 03 02 01   10 9 8 7 6 5 4 3

To my parents, Bob and Sue Hucke

To David Jones and Brandy Sargent

—M.H.

For Dolores M. Bielski

—U.B.

O reader, then behold and see!
As we are now, so you must be.

—Joseph Henshaw
Horae Sucissive

CONTENTS

Foreword...xi
Preface...xv
Acknowledgments...xvii

Introduction...3

I. NORTH

City North...11

Chicago City Cemetery...11
Graceland Cemetery...13
Jewish Graceland Cemetery...31
Wunder's Cemetery...33
St. Boniface Cemetery...34
Rosehill Cemetery...37
St. Henry Cemetery...49
Montrose Cemetery...51
Bohemian National Cemetery...53
Beth-El Cemetery...62
Ridgelawn Cemetery...62

Metro North...65

Calvary Cemetery...65
Church of the Holy Comforter...69
Fort Sheridan Cemetery...69
Memorial Park Cemetery...70
St. Adalbert Cemetery...71
Sunset Memorial Park...76
All Saints Cemetery...77
Shalom Memorial Park...78

II. WEST

City West...83

All Saints Polish National Catholic Cemetery...83
St. Nicholas Ukrainian Cemetery...84
St. John's/St. Johannes Cemetery...85
Rest Haven Cemetery...85
Cook County Poor Farm and Insane Asylum...87
Robinson Woods Indian Burial Ground...88
Westlawn Cemetery...89
Acacia Park Cemetery...91
Irving Park Cemetery...94
Mount Olive Cemetery...95

Metro West...99

St. Joseph Cemetery...99
Elmwood Cemetery...101
Forest Home/German Waldheim Cemetery...102
Jewish Waldheim Cemetery...112
Woodlawn Cemetery...117
Concordia Cemetery...118
Altenheim Cemetery...120
Mount Auburn Cemetery...120
Mount Emblem Cemetery...121
Elm Lawn Cemetery...121
Arlington Cemetery...122
Oak Ridge Cemetery...123
Mount Carmel Cemetery...125
Queen of Heaven Cemetery...134
Hinsdale Animal Cemetery...141

III. SOUTH

City South...147

Oak Woods Cemetery...147
Mount Olivet Cemetery...154
Mount Greenwood Cemetery...157
St. Casimir Cemetery...159

Metro South...163

Resurrection Cemetery...163
Bethania Cemetery...164
Lithuanian National Cemetery...165
Archer Woods Cemetery...167
Evergreen Cemetery...167
St. Mary Cemetery...168
Cedar Park Cemetery...169
Lincoln Cemetery...169
Oak Hill Cemetery...173
Mount Hope Cemetery...174
Restvale Cemetery...175
Holy Sepulchre Cemetery...176
Burr Oak Cemetery...178
St. Benedict Cemetery...179
Bachelors Grove Cemetery...180
St. James Cemetery...184
Mount Glenwood Cemetery...188
Holy Cross Cemetery...189

IV. BURIALS NOT IN CEMETERIES

Stephen A. Douglas Tomb...195
Yorktown Shopping Center...195
Mayslake/Francis S. Peabody...195
Cantigny/Robert R. McCormick...197
Jackson Park/Clarence Darrow...197
Wrigley Field/Steve Goodman...198

V. OUTLYING SITES

Masonic Cemetery/Robert Stroud...201
St. Sava Orthodox Monastery/Peter II...202
Monastery of the Most Holy Mother of God...202
Elk Grove Cemetery...202
Oakland Cemetery/Chester Gould...202

Appendix: List of Chicago Cemeteries...205

Bibliography...213
Index...219
About the Authors...229
Publisher's Credits...231

FOREWORD

When I was eight years old, my parents took me to Graceland Cemetery. It was my first visit to a cemetery; we were there because Graceland had some famous monuments and tombs. My only memory of that visit is of an ominous statue of death peering out through the shrubbery. It scared me enough that I never wanted to visit a cemetery again.

Some 21 years later, I visited Graceland Cemetery again. This time it was in conjunction with a class about urban history; we were visiting Graceland to see the monuments of people who had developed Chicago: George Pullman, Marshall Field, Potter Palmer, and their likes. I again saw "Death" or, as it is properly called, *Eternal Silence*, a statue by Lorado Taft. I lost my fear of visiting cemeteries at that moment and became to my friends a weird person who spent his free time exploring cemeteries. As a docent for the Chicago Architecture Foundation for 25 years, I have enjoyed sharing my interests in graveyards with Chicagoans and visitors from around the world.

As you read *Graveyards of Chicago*, you will be studying Chicago history and culture. As Ursula Bielski and Matt Hucke take you on a verbal tour to 70 cemeteries and seven other burial sites, they are encouraging you to visit these places and see for yourself what remarkable monuments we have here in Chicago. Paris, London, New York, and even Hollywood have had books written about their famous cemeteries, and the famous and infamous of their societies. *Graveyards of Chicago* is the first book that does this for Chicago.

I do not want to contribute to Chicago's reputation as a "Windy City" by adding more boosterism, but we have needed a book like this for a long time. We need to know where our heroes—and we have many—and our villains—we have just as many—are buried. Cemeteries are the repositories of our past. We should study the past, and *Graveyards of Chicago* does just that.

This book tells of the giants who have created Chicago, from the heroes who marched in our city's parades, to the villains who crept through its back alleys. For those who just want to hear the gossip, this is your book too. The anecdotes are plentiful enough to spice up any conversation about Chicago.

In reading this book, you will notice that cemeteries are layers of history. We recognize the famous people first and relate them to the periods of Chicago growth: Kinzie of the pioneer period, Cyrus H. McCormick of the prairie period, Marshall Field and Potter Palmer of the Growth of the Great Metropolis, and Richard W. Sears and Montgomery Ward of the modern period, the enterprising leaders of economic Chicago. We see the builders and planners of the physical Chicago: Burnham and Wacker of the Great Plan of 1909; Mies van der Rohe, William Le Baron Jenney, and John W. Root, the architects. We can see the political giants, Harold Washington and Richard J. Daley, and the political movers, Hinky Dink and Bathhouse John. There are the sports icons like George Halas, Adrian "Cap" Anson, Jack Johnson, Charles Comiskey, Buck Weaver, and Jesse Owens, who put Chicago in the sports headlines. And even those who regrettably put Chicago on the crime map, Al Capone and others of that sort, also played an important part in Chicago's past.

At the same time, these same cemeteries are the repositories of other larger trends. The immigration and migration of people into Chicago is shown by the names of the people buried in the city and suburban cemeteries. These stones record the waves of newcomers who shaped Chicago's neighborhoods.

Our cemeteries are also places of art. We know of their funerary art, but the art shown also in the stones and monuments, and especially the mausoleums, reflects the changing fashions and tastes in styles and building materials over the years. The Getty and Ryerson tombs by Louis Sullivan are but two such great works of art.

I hope that you will be intrigued enough to leave your armchair and visit these sites, especially on a clear, warm summer day. *Graveyards of Chicago* provides the starting point for finding those people who transformed Chicago—in less than 200 years—from a small trading post on the edge of a swamp to the magnificent city of today.

—WILLIAM Q. LUCAS
Chicago Architecture Foundation

PREFACE

Having made my dubious fortune as a so-called ghosthunter, it is likely that readers familiar with my writing will view this present effort as a morbid one, fueled by an unhealthy interest in all things dead and buried. Yet, quite to the contrary, my own interest in cemeteries springs most emphatically—and quite naturally, from a frantic interest in the business of living.

Chicago is often called a city of neighborhoods, but what of these silent boroughs? As we attend to the daily grind, millions sleep the eternal sleep all over the city, scattered like gems over the urban landscape. Giants of achievement from every walk of life share our zip codes, disregarded though they are by the more animated denizens that still pay taxes and vote. We often err in assuming that our local burial grounds are the hushed reflection of the communities that confine them; rather, urban cemeteries have little to do with the settling of the surrounding regions. In Chicago, as elsewhere, most 19th and early-20th century ossuaries were purposely founded in outlying, rural areas, accessed with some difficulty by funeral parties and mourners via railroad from the city center. With rare exceptions, ethnic populations did not migrate to settle near their common burial grounds; instead, the communities surrounding the city's cemeteries are primarily the incidental overflow of a burgeoning metropolis. Urban cemetery populations, then, are almost always necessarily displaced ones. But they are also needlessly disenfranchised.

This book is intended to serve at least three needs.

First, the need of the directly bereaved—native Chicagoans—for an awareness of the environments in which their loved ones have been laid to rest. So many have sent their dearly departed to area cemeteries with little or no perception of the history and company involved. A knowledge of both certainly compliments the funeral ritual, but also—perhaps more importantly—infuses the fact of death with the sense of comfort attainable only by historical perspective.

Second, the need of locals for an awareness of cemeteries as part of their communities—of cemetery residents as their literal neighbors. So often, Chicago's sprawling burial grounds are thought of only as massive acreages that must be circumvented in order to get where one is going. Ignoring the hundreds, sometimes thousands or hundreds of thousands, residing within their walls, Chicagoans essentially ignore some of the more stellar citizenry: Marshall Field, right over the fence from one's 16-unit Uptown apartment building. Richard Warren Sears, a stone's throw from the corner beef stand. And in the middle of the night, while south siders sleep, blues master Howlin' Wolf is sleeping too, just down the street and across the road.

Finally, this book is intended to add to our awareness of a larger, common history, for the greatest need of all is our culture's desperate need to increase its self-awareness. Chicago cemeteries are home to millions of contributors to our history and character, famous in both the standard sense and in so-called little ways. Yet, though we pay homage to the products of geniuses: architecture, art, dance, invention, merchandising, settlement, etc., we too often overlook the geniuses themselves. While we sing the praises of the great lights of our culture, we would do well to remember that these geniuses are still with us in a very real way, tucked into any of a billion plots in a thousand cemeteries around the globe. These places are more than mere boneyards. Though they exist most generically to house tangible remains, they are what they indeed are—showplaces of art and architecture, breathtaking expanses of landscape perfection, surprising refuges of nature and silence—because of the personalities that, at least for a while, miraculously infused blood and muscle with the will to survive—not physically, certainly, but through the immortality of achievement.

—Ursula Bielski

ACKNOWLEDGMENTS

I have benefited greatly from discussion of cemeteries world-wide in a mailing list hosted by Joel Gazis-Sax. His "City of the Silent" Web site was one of the first graveyard pages and continues to be among the most useful. Emperor Norton would be proud to have Joel in his service.

Larry Kestenbaum, maintainer of "The Political Graveyard" Web site, has provided a list of dead politicians and their burial sites, which I would often consult when visiting a Chicago graveyard for the first time. Jim Tipton's "Find-A-Grave" site is a valuable tool for locating other notable figures. Cat Yronwode's "Lucky Mojo" archive contains vast amounts of information on sacred sites and esoteric and Masonic symbolism. I'd also like to thank Katie Karrick for sending me her excellent print magazine, *Tomb With a View.*

Thanks to those who have contributed to online discussions of Chicago graveyards: Audrey Peters, Frank Kennedy, Mike Odahowski, Frank and Carla Martinek, Tina Leimer, and all others who participated in the "Graveyards of Chicago" news-group.

The Chicago Historical Society, the Evanston Historical Society, and the Rogers Park/West Ridge Historical Society have been invaluable in learning the history of Chicago cemeteries, particularly those that have disappeared.

I'd like to thank Dale Kaczmarek and the Ghost Research society for allowing me to participate in several explorations of haunted cemeteries and other haunted sites. Dale has been a serious investigator of the supernatural for over 25 years, and his knowledge of Chicago hauntings is superb.

Ghost researcher Troy Taylor has written extensively about ghosts and strange phenomena in the Chicago area.

I've learned much about Chicago cemeteries from historian Helen Sclair, who gave me some excellent suggestions when I first started exploring graveyards. Tom Berry of Calvary Cemetery and Bert and Jan Gast of Gast Monuments have also provided insights into local cemetery history.

I'd like to thank my friends who have tolerated and encouraged my interest in graveyards: David Diaz, Don Sitterley, John Sullivan, David Howell, Jim Morse, David Jones, Brandy Sargent, and Kevin Gutteron (who now knows nearly everyone buried at Rosehill).

My graveyard research began with a Web site, which would have never existed except for Matt Versaggi and Mark Cole, who donated the use of their servers to the cause.

The most helpful person I have encountered in my travels through Chicago graveyards has been David Wendell. While at Rosehill, he gave me several private tours of one of Chicago's finest historic cemeteries and recommended numerous other sites to visit and people to look for. The events he has organized have done a great deal to increase public appreciation of cemeteries.

Thanks, too, go to William Lucas, a longtime cemetery docent for the Chicago Architecture Foundation, for reviewing our manuscript, offering suggestions, and writing a wonderful foreword for the book.

Finally, I extend my deepest thanks to the two people who have most contributed to the success of this project: author Ursula Bielski, who graciously volunteered to convert my collection of facts into a well-written narrative and added a great deal of her own knowledge; and publisher Sharon Woodhouse, who conceived this project, kept it alive, and worked tirelessly to ensure that it would see print.

—MATT HUCKE

Despite our intentions, this book is far from comprehensive. In fact, it could be described most accurately as an introduction—an invitation to begin excavating the endless surprises buried with our bereaved urbanity. Such digging could go on forever; the determined have a staggering number of resources to exhaust in their quest for a comprehensive knowledge of Chicago's cemeteries.

A few souls, however, have made commendable progress in this regard, among them co-author Matt Hucke, whose "Graveyards of Chicago" Web site provides an ever-growing cache of photos and information on local cemeteries both dazzling and dilapidated. And many Chicagoans know local historian Helen Sclair as "The Cemetery Lady," owing to her longtime devotion to the discovery and dissemination of funerary facts. Sclair regularly shares her wealth of knowledge in formal seminars offered at Chicago's Newberry Library. For the fidgety, the Chicago Architecture Foundation conducts tours of a number of the city's architecturally and historically significant cemeteries, including Rosehill and its Mausoleum, Graceland, and Oak Woods.

Rugged individuals might fare quite well with local resources; cemeteries themselves often provide maps and guides, and some even publish books or booklets detailing the achievements of their residents. A number of such titles are detailed at the back of this book. Branch libraries and archives, too, contain untold literary treasures, as well as historical documents invaluable for the independent cemetery historian. Local historical societies and associations often house libraries rife with books, plot maps, and burial records, and genealogical societies will often assist researchers in locating death records, obituaries, genealogies, and settlement information. Ethnic societies, too, maintain similar resources for use in documenting the settlement of their specific cultures; cemetery histories and records often make up a substantial part of their holdings.

Finally, a number of online resources should be explored, including the aforementioned "Graveyards of Chicago" Web site; Cook County, IL GenWeb Research Resources—for expansive genealogical and general cemetery information; the site maintained by the Catholic Cemeteries of Chicago; and, for hours of fun, the intriguing "Find-a-Grave" site that efficiently traces the plots of hundreds—thousands?—of notable and notorious personalities around the world.

Owing to the the staggering amount of information on the subject, my own scholarly tour of Chicago's cemeteries was certainly no cake walk. In addition to scouring the above resources for seemingly endless minutiae, I relied on a number of individuals for both scraps and heaping helpings of information and assistance in completing the final manuscript, among them Brandon Zamora, whose diligent research efforts brought so much life to the personalities remembered in these pages; Anne Fitzpatrick, who located for me a number of elusive personalities through her endless resourcefulness; Dagmar Bradac, who graciously procured and bravely loaned a precious volume of information on Bohemian National Cemetery; Augie Alesky, who sent from his Centuries and Sleuths bookstore in Oak Park a guidebook on Forest Home and Waldheim Cemeteries to aid us in our cause; Dolores Bielski, who clipped dozens of newspaper and magazine articles related to our subject and kindly shared her own books on Graceland Cemetery; and, most overwhelmingly, David Wendell, whose inexhaustible stores of information could fill at least a hundred volumes.

In preparing the finished tome, the usual suspects deserve every accolade: David Cowan, for his initial readings of the manuscript, Bruce Clorfene for his editing prowess, Tim Kocher for his consistently wonderful design work, William Lucas for taking the time to get involved in our project and pen a foreword for it, and of course, Sharon Woodhouse, whose skill in every aspect of publishing continues to astound me.

Finally, gratitude is eternally due to my late father, Adalbert S. Bielski, who—when I was ten years old—opened up a whole new world by giving me driving lessons in Graceland Cemetery.

—Ursula Bielski

GRAVEYARDS OF CHICAGO

The prince, who kept the world in awe,
The judge, whose dictate fix'd the law,
The rich, the poor, the great, the small,
Are levell'd: death confounds 'em all.

—Gay, *Fables*

Rosehill Cemetery's well-known monument of Lulu Fellows,
who died in 1883 at age 16. Her headstone reads:
Many hopes lie buried here.

INTRODUCTION

My first visit to a Chicago graveyard was shortly after first arriving here in 1993. The book *Sweet Home Chicago* opened with a list of Chicago's "other" top ten attractions, one of which was Graceland Cemetery. It was this that prompted me to take the "L" train to the Sheridan Road stop one weekend during my first month in the city, then walk to Graceland. I had come to see the graves of the millionaires—Marshall Field, Potter Palmer, Henry Getty, etc.—but, lacking a map, walked in the wrong direction in the cemetery. It was there that I unexpectedly came across a most unusual grave, a glass box with a remarkably lifelike statue of a young girl inside.

Although considerably impressed by my encounter with Inez Clarke, I did not visit any cemeteries again for a couple of years. In late 1995 I read of Bachelors Grove, a tiny graveyard near the southwest suburb of Midlothian that was said to be one of the most haunted locations in the country, if not the world. I had always been fascinated with ghosts, though of a skeptical nature, so this seemed to be the perfect opportunity to witness a haunting—if in fact there was anything there. Thus, in the early spring of 1996, I set forth to explore the haunted graveyard. I drove nearly two hours, then walked along a path into the forest to the small abandoned cemetery, growing more fearful as it came into view. I thought that, at last, I would see a ghost and be convinced that they exist.

Nothing happened.

A few months later, I happened to drive past Rosehill, and looking for a quiet place to relax, ventured inside. I explored the area around the grave of Leonard Volk and was repeatedly surprised by the diversity, quality, and ingenuity of the monuments and mausoleums there. Rosehill possessed charm, character, and atmosphere, and I decided then that I should begin regular trips to Chicago cemeteries until I had seen them all. In the following weeks I returned to Graceland (this time with a camera), Rosehill, Jewish Graceland, and Calvary. I went as far afield as Resurrection, home to Chicago's best-known ghost story, and visited Forest Home and Mt. Carmel whenever my work took me to the western suburbs.

In August of 1996 I created the Web site "Graveyards of Chicago," a name that was primarily chosen because the domain *graveyards.com* was available. The site originally featured about 20 photos from Graceland, Rosehill, and Calvary. (It has since grown to include over 600 photos from more than 20 cemeteries.)

In the summer of 1997 I was contacted by Ursula Bielski, author of the soon-to-be-published *Chicago Haunts: Ghostly Lore of the Windy City*, who wished to use several of my photographs. The publisher of that book, Sharon Woodhouse, then invited me to write *Graveyards of Chicago*. With the addition of Ursula's writing skills, the book has evolved into far more than simply a printed version of the Web site.

In my explorations, I have come to appreciate the beauty of old graveyards. Older cemeteries have much more interesting monuments than modern cemeteries, which tend to be vast expanses of nearly identical flat granite markers. This uniformity came about shortly after World War I. Before then, the monuments were as varied as the individuals they commemorated. Any old graveyard, even the smaller ones, is likely to have a wide variety of different monument types. While simple rectangular slabs are the most common, you will also find sarcophagi, ledgers (flat grave covers), obelisks, statues (upright, seated, reclining), angels, urns, crosses and crucifixes, cylinders, cubes, stone trees, books, lecterns, columns, and others that defy categorization. Mausoleums show as much variety as monuments do—they may be freestanding, attached to neighboring tombs, built into the side of a hill or almost entirely underground, flat-roof, peaked-roof, domed, pyramidal, adorned with columns, angels, lions, or sphinxes.

Most cemeteries welcome visitors. Observe the posted closing hours, take care not to damage monuments or vegetation, and be respectful of the living and the dead.

—Matt Hucke

I. NORTH

An angel monument in St. Boniface Cemetery.

CITY NORTH

Montrose Cemetery's striking memorial to the 600 people
who perished in the 1903 Iroquois Theatre Fire.

The mausoleum of Ira Couch near North Avenue in Lincoln Park, on the grounds of the Chicago Historical Society, is the last visible remnant of Chicago's City Cemetery.

CHICAGO CITY CEMETERY

Lincoln Park
Behind the Chicago Historical Society
Clark Street & North Avenue
Chicago

It seems that nearly every Chicagoan, and many a tourist for
   that matter, is aware that native businessman **Ira Couch**
(1806-1857) is dead, though almost no one knows exactly who
he was, what he did, or why, for heaven's sake, his tomb stands
in the middle of Lincoln Park. For generations, drivers along the
park's rich sweep of green have ogled the hotelkeeper and
realtor's somber tomb with a mixture of keen curiosity and frank
unease, wondering at the explanation for this odd ornament
affixed in the backyard of the Chicago Historical Society. The
answer is disappointingly unmysterious.

   Unknown to many natives and most tourists is the fact that
the public playground that is today's Lincoln Park was once the
civic cemetery. This aptly named Chicago City Cemetery
stretched from Armitage Avenue south to the then city limits,
providing temporary homes for 20,000 dearly departed prairie-
dwellers. Most of these were later disinterred and relocated to
various sites around the city upon the closing of City Cemetery
around 1870. When this mass evacuation began, the Couch
family rallied and appealed to officials to let Ira remain due to
the cost of transporting the mausoleum to another site. In time,
the city consented, and Ira Couch remains where he is for the
simple reason that his tomb would have been too expensive to
move.

   Before the establishment of City Cemetery, Chicago had
made some poor decisions concerning the question of burial. The
area's first homesteaders had buried their kin in their backyards,
leading to a few surprises later on when the downtown area was
dug up to lay the foundations for skyscrapers and other develop-
ments. In addition, the Chicago River sometimes played tricks on

the bereaved who might bid farewell to their loved ones only to watch them floating by on the waterway some time later, having been purged from their graves after a particularly heavy rain. Further, the two cemeteries that were finally established in 1835—a Protestant one at Chicago and Michigan avenues and a Catholic one near 23rd Street and Calumet Avenue—were both situated squarely on the lake shore, leading to the frequent unearthing of caskets. When population increases added to the inadequacy of the funerary system, the city selected an acreage at Clark Street and North Avenue on which to found Chicago City Cemetery. Simultaneously, the Roman Catholic Diocese of Chicago secured for its faithful a portion of property between Dearborn and State streets, south of North Avenue. Though none of this land was exactly towering above the water table, any of it was preferable to the shaky sepulchers of the beachfront burial grounds. The transfer of bodies to the new sites began at once.

Scarcely a decade after the opening of the new cemeteries, however, Chicagoans began to loudly complain about them. Besides the overcrowding resulting from both population growth and a string of cholera epidemics, echoes of earlier days could be heard in the fear that inadequate burials were leading to increased disease and contamination of the water. Fueling this near panic was the fact that the city morgue, as well as a holding building for epidemic victims, the so-called Pest House, were both located on the Chicago City Cemetery grounds. By the mid-1850s, concerned congregations and families were beginning to move their loved ones to "safer" sites, and by the early 1870s, City Cemetery was closed.

After all the unpleasant lessons had been learned, Chicago went about its business secure in the belief that Lincoln Park's posh property was virtually corpse-free, except for the tidy tomb of Mr. Couch and the unmarked grave of **David Kennison** (1736-1852), who claimed to be a 116-year-old Boston Tea Party survivor. In 1970, however, bones from City Cemetery were found during the building of an addition to the Chicago Historical Society, and in 1986, reality was once again given a blow by the uncovering of 15 bodies during construction at the Streeterville site of one of Chicago's two earliest lakefront cemeteries.

GRACELAND CEMETERY

4001 North Clark Street
Chicago
773/525-1105
Est. 1860

When real estate investor Thomas B. Bryan founded Graceland Cemetery in 1860, the now-bustling neighborhood was practically wilderness. Over the years, a number of architects and designers worked to civilize this 120-acre enclosure, in typical Chicago fashion. Bryan's nephew, Bryan Lathrop, served as president of the cemetery for a number of years and was enchanted by naturalism. As a result, architects William Le Baron Jenney and Ossian Cole Simonds were hired to enhance the enclosure. Simonds was so taken with the project that he ended up turning his professional attention fully towards landscape design. Through the work he did at Graceland and afterward, Simonds anticipated the gracious natural appreciation of the Prairie School artists.

At Graceland, not only the landscape can be credited to Chicago's architectural geniuses. More obvious contributions can be found in the several buildings and monuments on the property. Visitors enter gates designed by acclaimed local firm Holabird & Roche, who also created the administration building and waiting room near the entrance, as well as the cemetery's chapel, which includes the city's oldest crematorium, circa 1893.

A walk through Graceland will bring the visitor in close contact with thousands of Chicago's most influential personalities, including some of the city's earliest residents and most aggressive civic leaders.

John Kinzie (1763-1828), the much-maligned "first white settler" of the Chicago area, was taken ill with apoplexy on January 6, 1828, while living with his family at the home of John Beaubien, just south of Fort Dearborn. His body was originally buried north of the river. Later, however, his body was disinterred and transferred first to the old north side cemetery, then to City Cemetery, and finally to its current location at Graceland, miles north of the fledgling settlement he had known.

A Quebec native, Kinzie was born several years before the American Revolution, traveling in adulthood to the prairie along the southwestern shores of Lake Michigan and settling across the river from Fort Dearborn. The Kinzies occupied the homestead originally built by Jean Baptiste DuSable, the first true permanent settler of the area, where they lived until the Fort Dearborn Massacre of 1812. By fleeing to Michigan, they escaped the fate of their fellow settlers and soldiers who were butchered on the sands. Several years later, Kinzie returned to the site to reclaim his land and resume his trade.

Chicago's first wheeler-dealer died in 1828. But the Chicago he left behind had only just begun. The relentless business sense of Kinzie was echoed in the lives of hundreds of entrepreneurs who followed his lead in exploiting the rich resources, geographical and human, of the burgeoning city on the lake. A good number of those financial wizards join Kinzie at Graceland.

Chicago women were among the first to be smitten with a new concept in shopping, the department store, flocking to bustling State Street to patronize a remarkable retail institution, the darling of merchandising king **Marshall Field** (1834-1906). Guiding the venture to the top as the largest wholesale and retail dry goods dealer in the world, Field became the richest man in Chicago, worth an estimated $120 million.

Field's final days were filled with sorrow after the shooting of his son, Marshall Field II in November 1905. Ruled an accidental death by the coroner, rumors nevertheless spread that it was either a suicide or the result of a brawl in the Everleigh Club, a luxurious brothel of local infamy. The elder Marshall Field never recovered from his grief, died of pneumonia three months later, and went to his rest at Graceland, where he reposes with four generations of Fields. His monument was created by noted sculptor Daniel Chester French, who later designed the Lincoln Memorial in Washington D.C.

Maine-bred piano and organ manufacturer **William Kimball** (1828-1904) began his life in Chicago as a traveling salesman intrigued by the opportunity offered by this burgeoning metropolis. Anticipating a lively future here for the arts, Kimball settled in Chicago and set up a piano and organ dealership. His success led him to open an organ factory, and demand soon added pianos to his list of products. He was successful enough to be counted among the cream of Chicago society, living out his days in a million-dollar mansion at the corner of 18th Street and Prairie Avenue, in the heart of the city's most exclusive residential district.

Philip D. Armour (1832-1901), one of Chicago's meat-packing giants, created his empire by selling canned pork to the Union Army during the Civil War. In 1875, he moved his Milwaukee-based business to Chicago, where he began shipping fresh meat across the country in refrigerated train cars and exporting canned meat to the entire world. Armour was a very religious man, and after a particularly moving sermon entitled, "If I Had a Million Dollars," he gave $1 million to Reverend Frank Gunsaulus, who founded the Armour Institute, which was later to become the Illinois Institute of Technology. His Graceland monument is an immense rectangular solid of grey granite on a three-tiered base.

George Pullman (1831-1897) was buried securely by a family terrified that his body would be snatched by the railroad emperor's incensed ex-employees, most of whom had lost their jobs at the end of the infamous 1894 Pullman Strike. Dying only three years after the event, which was forcefully "settled" by federal troops, George's body was encased in a coffin, sealed in a block of concrete, and covered with an extra ton of concrete and railroad ties. Over this extraordinarily well-protected corpse rises a mighty Corinthian column flanked by curving stone benches, a monument designed by Solon Beman, architect of the company town of Pullman (later annexed to the south side of Chicago).

Ironically, the body of a hated oppressor was given the same protection as that of a beloved liberator: President Lincoln is likewise entombed in a block of concrete in downstate Springfield.

The **Goodman Family** monument provides a dramatic over-

Department store multimillionaire Marshall Field lies in a grave watched
over by *Memory,* the work of Lincoln sculptor Daniel Chester French
(*above*). Brilliant white marble Corinthian columns surround the grave
of William Kimball, piano manufacturer, and his wife (*below*).

A mighty column stands over the enormous concrete block protecting
the body of railroad tycoon George Pullman (*above*). William Hulbert,
founder of the National League of professional baseball, rests
beneath this appropriately shaped headstone (*below*).

Potter Palmer and Bertha Honoré Palmer lived in a castle on North Lake
Shore Drive. Their eternal home is no less magnificent: a Greek-styled
temple with sixteen Ionic columns surrounding the granite sarcophagi of
the Palmers (*above*). Their children and grandchildren are buried beneath
the floor, and Bertha's parents are across the road. The Palmer sarcophagi
feature inverted torches, a Victorian symbol of mourning (*below*).

look that beckons visitors to spend a few moments gazing across the halcyon waters of Lake Willowmere. Lumber mogul William Goodman had the family mausoleum designed by architect friend, Howard Van Doren Shaw, upon the death of Goodman's son, Kenneth. A playwright, in training for a lieutenant's commission with the United States Navy, 35-year-old Kenneth was fatally stricken with influenza during the 1918 epidemic. Along with commissioning the handsome monument in his son's honor, Goodman also hired Shaw to create a memorial theater in the same style—the renowned Goodman Theatre adjoining the Art Institute of Chicago.

There is no debating the most prestigious cemetery in Chicago—Graceland—or the most prestigious site in that cemetery: the hilltop shrine to the memory of the Palmers. In death, as in life, **Potter** (1826-1902) and **Bertha Honoré** (1850-1918) Palmer bought themselves the center of attention. They rest beneath a breathtaking hilltop temple, also overlooking Lake Willowmere, that remains the last word in eternal digs, at least in Chicago. Hailing from New York, Palmer moved his dry-goods shop to Chicago's bustling Lake Street district. His concept of the money-back guarantee caused a sensation and won him a legion of loyal customers. Palmer was the originator of the now-widespread motto of businesses everywhere: "The customer is always right." After accumulating a king's ransom in profits, Palmer sold his store to Marshall Field and Levi Leiter, choosing to focus his efforts on real estate.

With the money to back up his wildest dreams, Palmer bought a street, State Street, aiming to create an entirely new business district. First, he widened the thoroughfare, then put up new buildings along its length, setting as its jewel a gorgeous luxury hotel. Dubbing it the Palmer House, Potter presented the hotel to new wife, Bertha, on the occasion of their marriage in 1871. A good year for weddings in Chicago, it was a poor one for real estate investments, and the Palmers watched their new commercial strip burn to the ground with the rest of the city in the Great Chicago Fire. Among the buildings destroyed was Palmer's new "marble palace" of commerce, a two-year-old building which he leased to Marshall Field. Still inspired, still loaded, and with the aid of the largest loan ever given to an individual at the time, Potter rebuilt everything, including the hotel, whose opulent elegance put its lavish predecessor to shame.

Once he had moved the center of Chicago's business, Palmer set his sights on moving the center of its society, from Prairie Avenue on the near south side, to the north side stretch of Lake Shore Drive at Oak Street where he erected the now-demolished Palmer Mansion.

One of the most photographed mausoleums at Graceland is the strangely eclectic tomb of the Schoenhofen family, a monstrous pyramid structure which houses the remains of German immigrant and master brewer, **Peter Schoenhofen** (1827-1893). The family became the victims of one of Chicago's most heated cases of property seizure when authorities discovered that the Schoenhofens retained and encouraged their Germanic ties. As a result, the family's possessions were whisked away. Some purport that Colonel Graf Schenk von Stauffenberg—the planter of the bomb in Hitler's bunker in July of 1944—was a descendant of Peter Schoenhofen. Schoenhofen's tomb, which combines Egyptian and Christian symbols, is based on a similar pyramid in Milan, Italy. Similar structures can be found in other American cities: the Brunswig mausoleum in New Orleans and the Van Ness/Parsons mausoleum in Brooklyn.

Not only business leaders rest at Graceland; the cemetery also gathers an impressive array of local public heroes. During his time in office, Illinois governor **John Peter Altgeld** (1847-1902) played a high-profile role in Chicago's unfolding history. First, Altgeld was highly criticized and even burned in effigy after his pardoning of the so-called Haymarket Martyrs. Undaunted by public opinion, he went on to defend the Pullman strikers the very next year, urging President Cleveland to refrain from breaking up the strike with federal troops. For his humanitarian efforts, Altgeld was himself branded an anarchist, a designation that guaranteed the end of his political career.

Charles Wacker (1856-1929) was a driving force behind the establishment of architect Daniel Burnham's Chicago Plan of 1909, which laid out the city on a grid, conceived traffic-relieving bi-leveled streets around the downtown area, and arranged for

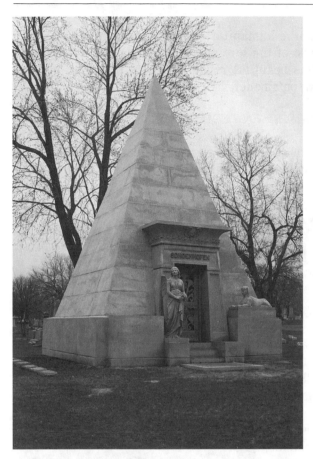

German brewer Peter Schoenhofen is entombed within this pyramid, guarded by an angel and a sphinx, a somewhat unusual combination. In the late nineteenth century, Egyptian symbology was associated with death because of recent archaeological discoveries.

the design of a group of large, scattered parks strung together by boulevards. Wacker served as chairman of the Plan Commission, laboring long and hard for the dollars and dedicated to making it a reality. When the Plan went through, Wacker's struggle was commemorated by the city, who named the new double-decker bank of the Chicago River after the man who had made this remarkable street and the rest of the Chicago Plan possible.

Graceland also boasts some of the most beautiful funerary art in the world. A popular and atypical example is the knight standing guard over the plot of *Chicago Daily News* publisher **Victor Lawson** (1850-1925). Designed by renowned sculptor Lorado Taft, the piece, entitled *Crusader*, was considered a fitting memorial to the humanitarian newspaperman, known for his creation and use of the foreign correspondent as a valuable news resource. This beautiful rendering bears no name, but is inscribed with Lawson's belief that

ABOVE ALL THINGS TRUTH BEARETH AWAY THE VICTORY.

Without question, Graceland's most familiar, and most photographed, memorial is another of Taft's masterpieces: the cloaked bronze rendering of *Eternal Silence*, popularly christened "The Statue of Death." Standing sentinel over **Dexter Graves** (1789-1844), a hotel owner and early settler, and his family, the figure has been called striking, haunting, frightening, morbid, imposing, foreboding. And rumor still has it that an unflinching gaze into its shrouded eyes will grant the beholder a vision of the afterworld.

Not only a memorial ground for local legends, Graceland boasts many national and international heroes as well. Farming was revolutionized when **Cyrus McCormick** (1809-1894) invented a machine which combined the separate tasks of earlier harvesters into one device. This reaper led farmers to more than double their crop sizes, and made McCormick a fortune. A Virginia native, Cyrus inherited the impetus toward invention from his father, who himself worked for many years, in vain, to create a mechanical reaper. When son Cyrus finally got it right, the younger McCormick patented the device and began producing copies of it in 1837. Over the next ten years, the popularity of the machine was so great that McCormick decided to build a factory in Chicago; he further boosted sales by sending door-to-door salesmen to peddle the reaper. A written guarantee and the promise of easy assembly won McCormick many customers, as well as a place among the great inventors cited as exemplifiers of American ingenuity and the country's trial-and-error system of development.

Allan Pinkerton (1819-1884) was born in Glasgow, Scotland in the early 19th century. While in his twenties, he emigrated to the growing Chicago area and settled down to work as a barrel maker. At some point during this modest career, Pinkerton nabbed a gang of counterfeiters. An appreciative public saw fit to elect him sheriff, and so the dedicated Scotsman took the first step down a remarkable road.

In 1850, Pinkerton organized Pinkerton's National Detective Agency, becoming the first ever private detective; he was also appointed to the position of city detective in his adopted hometown. When Pinkerton recovered a burgled cache of money for the Adams Express Co., he won much adulation. Far greater praise, however, came in 1861, when the enterprising private eye uncovered a plot to murder Abraham Lincoln. Pinkerton went on to support Lincoln's government throughout the Civil War, organizing the U.S. Army's Secret Service. Just before his death in 1884, he published *Thirty Years a Detective*, in which he chronicled the unique experiences of his singular profession.

Near Pinkerton's grave is that of **Vincent Starrett** (1886-1974), *Chicago Tribune* columnist and founding member of The Baker Street Irregulars, the oldest and most prestigious of the many societies devoted to the appreciation of Sherlock Holmes.

Eighth Chief Justice of the U.S. Supreme Court **Melville Fuller** (1833-1910) was the first such appointee to have academic legal training, having attended Harvard Law School, for one year, during the mid-19th century.

Joining Fuller at Graceland is top Pinkerton employee and Civil War personality **Timothy Webster** (1821-1862), who was

Buried around a large obelisk are two mayors of Chicago, father and son: Carter Henry Harrison I, murdered 1893, and Carter Henry Harrison II.

hanged in Virginia after being convicted as a spy for the Union.

Alongside these early Chicago powerhouses, rest several Chicago mayors, including **Joseph Medill** (1823-1899), who won election on the "fireproof ticket"; **Carter Henry Harrison** (1825-1893), murdered in 1893 by a disgruntled office-seeker; and his son, **Carter Henry Harrison II** (1860-1953), the city's 30th and first Chicago-born mayor.

Near the graves of the two Mayors Harrison, is Graceland's most beautiful monument, the life-sized marble statue of young **Inez Clarke** (1873-1880), who died in 1880, which sits in a bronze-framed glass box. Many people stop to visit Inez, who seems much more pleasant than the millionaires and politicians that dominate this cemetery.

Sports historians and fans will search in vain for a stone commemorating the first black world heavyweight champion, **Jack Johnson** (1878-1946). When Johnson won the championship in 1908, angry whites were desperate to find someone, an elusive "Great White Hope," to reclaim the title. Enraged by Johnson's marriage to a white woman, the champ's enemies jeered him until 1915, when Johnson lost the title to Jess Willard. The devoted husband bought his wife, Etta, a plot in Graceland, marked by a large monument inscribed with their surname. But while Mrs. Johnson's grave is clearly identified, the prizefighter himself rests beside her in anonymity, despite offers of fans to put up a marker.

Though Johnson's marker is nonexistent, recognition of the

fight game may be found in the headstone of **Robert Fitzsimmons** (1862-1917), another boxing superstar, this one famous for his signature uppercut punch. An English native raised in New Zealand, Fitzsimmons held titles in three divisions, winning the middleweight title in 1891, the heavyweight title in 1897, and the light-heavyweight title in 1903. After his death, many new fans were won over by the endearing photos affixed to Fitzsimmons's flush stone, inscribed by his wife to *My Beloved Husband... World Champion*, until their recent theft.

And a whimsical stone baseball commemorates the life, and death, of **William A. Hulbert** (1832-1882), founder of the National League, who would be overjoyed to hear the crowds on the wind blowing out from Wrigley Field just a few blocks away.

Inez Clarke, age six, her likeness preserved forever in marble.

One of the most obviously represented of Graceland's diverse cultural groups is that of the architects who designed many of the site's most acclaimed mausoleums and markers, including their own.

The mausoleum of **Martin Ryerson** (1818-1887) was commissioned to architect Louis Henri Sullivan, who had envisioned a number of office buildings for the lumber merchant. Hulking and unornamented, the Ryerson structure seems nothing like its neighbor, the Getty Tomb, though this landmark was also designed by Sullivan for Ryerson's partner, **Henry Harrison Getty** (1838-

The Getty mausoleum (*above*), a "symphony in stone" by architect
Louis Henri Sullivan, has been designated a Chicago landmark.
Sullivan's headstone (*below*) features some of his own
geometric designs on the bronze front.

1920). Of this masterpiece of ornamentation, no lesser critic than Frank Lloyd Wright remarked, "Outside the realm of music, what finer requiem?"

Though he made priceless contributions to architecture and design, and left Chicago a thousand times more beautiful for his efforts, **Louis Sullivan** (1856-1924) joined his clients in Graceland with little more than his funeral suit to show for his work. At the time of his death, Sullivan's genius had fallen out of fashion, as popular taste reverted to classical styles. The prodigious architect received only one commission in his last year of life; his estate did not allow for even a grave marker. Those faithful to the beloved architect, however, later furnished his lot with a fitting headstone, designed by Thomas Tallmadge, who invented the term "Chicago School" in writing of the city's influential architects. In creating this tangible tribute to a true master, Tallmadge achieved a perfect reflection of Sullivan's work, embossing a large impressive stone with a profile of the architectural giant, along with an intricate geometric design characteristic of, and derived from, Sullivan's own renderings. The sides of the boulder-like stone are finely chiseled, demonstrating the harmony of the modern skyscraper with the natural world.

Incidentally, an adjacent section holds the grave of **Richard Nickel** (1928-1972), an architecture photographer who was accidentally killed during the demolition of the Chicago Stock Exchange while trying to preserve Sullivan's work.

Ludwig Mies van der Rohe's (1886-1969) "less is more" philosophy of design echoes for eternity through the utilitarian marker designed by his grandson, architect Dirk Lohan—an unpolished slab of black granite bearing only his bluntly-chiseled name.

László Moholy-Nagy (1895-1946), founder of the Chicago-based New Bauhaus, is buried beneath a nondescript flush stone near the cemetery chapel. Nearby, architect **Marion Mahony Griffin** (1871-1962) took Moholy-Nagy one step further: this grave is actually unmarked.

Also resting in peace here is **Dwight Perkins** (1867-1941), a Prairie School architect who aided in the establishment of the

Daniel Hudson Burnham favored classical architecture, but his
monument is a simple rough granite boulder. Burnham and his family
are the only burials on this small island, which is accessed by a simple
footbridge. The Palmer tomb can be seen in the distance.

Forest Preserve District of Cook County.

Architect **Daniel Burnham** (1846-1912), creator of the
universally acclaimed Chicago Plan of 1909, is buried with his
family on the little island afloat in Lake Willowmere, their
graves accessible to all by a concrete footbridge. One of the most
influential of the city's many architectural giants, Burnham designed a number of remarkable Chicago buildings, including the
Reliance Building and the landmark department store of Marshall Field & Co., and planned the legendary White City for the
Columbian Exposition of 1893. Yet he is most lauded today for
saving Chicago's lakefront from commercial and residential development. Even now, the miles of open, public shoreline, lined
with parks, a zoo, museums, bicycle trails, a golf course, even a
bird sanctuary, bear testimony to the unfathomable foresight of
Burnham's design. Because of his plan, Lake Michigan has remained the mysterious and intimate center of Chicago's identity.

The grave of Burnham's business partner, **John Wellborn Root** (1850-1891), is marked by a massive Celtic cross, uncharacteristically traditional except for a giveaway inset near the base, which bears Root's drawing of the entrance to the now-demolished Phoenix Building. Though most of Burnham & Root's work has disappeared from Chicago's landscape, two of their structures remain favorites among architecture aficionados: the Rookery at 209 South LaSalle Street and the Monadnock Building at Dearborn Street and Jackson Boulevard. The latter marked the end of one engineering road: at 16 stories, it is the tallest building that could be designed using the old load-bearing walls.

Near Root is the massive pink granite monument of architect **Peirce Anderson** (1870-1924), inset with a bronze carving of the deceased's face. Anderson worked with Daniel Burnham before helping to found the architectural firm of Graham, Anderson, Probst and White. The only writing this stunning grave-marker bears is Anderson's name cut into the bronze in letters less than an inch tall.

Architecture's new road was forged by Graceland resident **William Le Baron Jenney** (1832-1907), inventor of the sky-scraper. Frustrated by the height limitations imposed by load-bearing walls, Jenney masterminded the skeleton frame and first used the concept in designing the Home Insurance Building, which, at ten stories, towered over the intersection of LaSalle and Adams streets when it was built in 1884. Unfortunately, the pioneer structure was demolished in 1931, but modern architecture is everywhere, especially in Chicago, haunted by its memory.

A final destination here for architecture fans is the grave of thoroughly modern designer, **Fazlur Rahman Khan** (1929-1982), whose work with Skidmore, Owings and Merrill brought both the Sears Tower and John Hancock Building to Chicago's dramatic skyline.

Weed-choked sarcophagi at Jewish Graceland (*above*). This road
(*below*) passes behind stone curbing that marks the borders of
the plots, something forbidden at most modern cemeteries.

JEWISH GRACELAND CEMETERY
3919 North Clark Street
Chicago
Jewish, Est. 1850s

Before 1880, Jewish immigrants could count on American encouragement of their settlement and aspirations toward success. In later years, however, new Jewish arrivals in Chicago and other cities faced a cool reception at best and open hostility at worst. In this city, some of the most contrary reactions to these new settlers from Eastern Europe came from the Jews already situated here: the well-assimilated German-speaking Jews who considered the new wave of immigrants provincial, conservative, and mortifyingly foreign.

Jacob Gottlieb, Chicago's first Jewish settler, had ventured to the city in the late 1830s. He was one of the minority of Jewish immigrants to the United States who traveled west of the East Coast; in Chicago, he and a handful of others settled on the edge of what is now the Loop, near Lake and Wells streets, living above or near their businesses. A dozen years after Gottlieb's arrival, the Jewish population exploded. Between 1850 and 1860, Gottlieb gained 1,400 new Jewish neighbors, who settled LaSalle, Randolph, and Clark streets and areas north of the Chicago River.

As the numbers and economic status of these German-Jews climbed, the necessity for a communal burial ground became evident. In the mid-1840s, the Jewish Burial Ground Society was founded, its directors first purchasing lots in the old City Cemetery, and then in the nearby town of Lake View, where three acres were set up at what is now Belmont Avenue and Clark Street.

Though limited space necessitated the transplanting of this first Jewish burial ground west to what is now Addison Street and Narragansett Avenue, another early Jewish cemetery remains in the Lakeview neighborhood today. In the 1850s, a group of bankers formed the Hebrew Benevolent Society to furnish medical and funerary benefits for its membership.

The site is today part of the burial ground unofficially known as Jewish Graceland, located immediately adjacent to Wunder's Cemetery, south of Graceland along Clark Street. Here are graves from a number of congregations that purchased sections after its founding, among them Kehilath Anshe Mayriv, the Congregation of the Sons of Peace, and Shebra Kadisha Ubikar Cholm. Once partitioned by fences, the sections are today undivided and indistinguishable.

Jewish Graceland's obelisks are still majestic amidst the cemetery's disrepair of recent years.

Compared to the closely-clipped and pricey elegance of "nonsectarian" Graceland, the site known as Jewish Graceland seems primitive and impoverished. In fact, Jewish Graceland boasts only one family mausoleum: that of the **Hyman** family, a 1928 structure that towers over the modest markers of this densely populous, increasingly wild landscape.

Jewish Graceland's disrepair of recent years includes damage to a number of the monuments. A cluster of cylinders belonging to the **Meyer** family has been one victim of this type of neglect, with the largest of their cylinders toppled from its lofty pedestal, and a marble sculpture of a woman's face lost entirely.

WUNDER'S
3963 North Clark Street
Chicago
773/525-4038
Protestant

During the reign of the old City Cemetery, a number of members of First Saint Paul's Evangelical and Reformed Church

owned lots on the property. When City Cemetery was closed, exhumations from this communal plot formed the basis of Wunder's Cemetery, named for pastor Henry Wunder, also situated at Clark Street and Irving Park Road and divided by fencing from so-called Jewish Graceland to the south.

Visitors to Wunder's will find sure traces of the cemetery's heritage. As the oldest Germanic Protestant cemetery in the city, many of the 19th-century markers at Wunder's bear inscriptions in German.

Commonly called "The Sisters," Wunder's one monument under glass is unusually elaborate for a cemetery of this size.

ST. BONIFACE CEMETERY

4901 North Clark Street
Chicago
773/238-3106
Catholic, Est. 1863

The St. Boniface cenotaph, near a priests' section of this cemetery.

A bit further north of the cemetery cluster at Clark Street and Irving Park Road is another urban ethnic burial ground, this one founded by German Roman Catholics.

Like most ethnic populations of the 19th century, Germans harbored intense prejudices. In this case, the disdain of German Catholics for their Irish brethren led to Germans' refusal to be buried with these Celtic congregants at the Diocesan cemetery, Calvary, in Evanston. With no other place to send their dead, German Catholic congregations at the Diocesan churches of St. Joseph, St. Francis, St. Michael, and St. Peter founded the German Roman Catholic Saint Boniface Cemetery Association to provide burial space and services exclusively for Roman Catholics of German origin, with any surplus revenue to be used for charitable purposes. This benevolent policy is evident in the contrast between St. Boniface and Calvary, the latter of which re-invested surplus funds in itself and, as a result, boasts one of the metropolitan area's most stunning entrance arches, as opposed to the simple iron entry gate of St. Boniface.

The cemetery commemorates the legend of its namesake

with a **cenotaph** honoring the 8th-century Boniface, who requested permission from Pope Gregory II to convert the pagans of Thuringia (now a state in Germany). Once among them, the missionary priest aimed to dem-onstrate the authority of the Christian God. Chopping down a tree sacred to Thor, Boniface watched confidently as the pieces of wood fell into the shape of a cross, underscoring his message of Christian salvation. For his efforts and faith, the missionary won many Germanic converts to the Church, becoming known as the Apostle of Germany. Here in this Chicago cemetery, Boniface's memorial watches over the graves of area priests buried around the marker.

One of only two mausoleums in St. Boniface. A pair of saints guards the entrance, over which is the winged face of a cherub.

Other popular destinations here are the cemetery's **Civil War Monument** and a memorial dedicated to members of the German singing society, **The Maennerchor.**

Granite sarcophagi.

The castellated Gothic entrance to Rosehill cemetery (*above*),
by W.W. Boyington, architect of the Chicago Water Tower.
(*Below*) The Egyptian-styled mausoleum of Darius Miller. Note
the winged scarabs near the roof and the elaborate column capitals.

ROSEHILL CEMETERY
5800 North Ravenswood Avenue
Chicago
773/561-5940
Est. 1859

In 1867, Dr. I. Chronic, a prestigious German scholar and rabbi, contracted with Rosehill Cemetery for a portion of its holdings, initiating Chicago's first Jewish burials in a non-Jewish cemetery. One of the pioneering Reform rabbis in the United States who worked to replace the traditional Saturday Sabbath with Sunday observance, Dr. Chronic was locally known for his creation of the first Jewish publication in Chicago, the monthly *Zeichen der Zeit* or "Signs of the Times."

When Rosehill, the largest nonsectarian cemetery in the Chicago metropolitan area, was established in the mid 19th Century, the 350-acre site sprawled almost five miles north of the city limits. Funeral parties traveled to it by renting special cars from the Chicago & North Western railroad, which ran a spur line from the heart of the city to the Rosehill gates. Today, the enormous expanse is surrounded by neighborhoods, circumvented by buses and taxis, and generally ignored by local residents, whose primary concern is how to get around the cemetery during rush hour.

After the C&NW tracks were elevated around the turn of the century, a new station was built at the Rosehill entrance, along with a casket elevator, whose tower is still visible. Both were designed to harmonize with the cemetery's signature entrance, built five years after its opening. The entry's architect, **W.W. Boyington** (1818-1898), himself an eternal occupant of Rosehill, celebrated the site with a limestone portal of castellated Gothic magnificence, which hinted at his later, now famous design of the Chicago Water Tower.

Take a walk through these gates and find yourself among the who's who of Chicago history: Rosehill is home to **Ignaz**

Schwinn (1860-1948), bicycle king; **Otis Ward Hinckley** (1861-1924) and **George Schmitt** (1866-1931), water magnates; **Robert S. Scott**, colleague of Carson and Pirie; **George W. Maher** (1864-1926), architect; **Aaron Montgomery Ward** (1843-1913), mail order pioneer; **Julius Rosenwald** (1862-1932), financial genius behind Sears, Roebuck & Co. and founder of the Museum of Science and Industry; **Richard Warren Sears** (1863-1914) himself; and thousands of other hometown movers and shakers.

Travelers on Chicago's streets will recognize a number of namesakes here as well: **Hoyne**, **Wells**, **Peterson**, **Kedzie**.

Inventors, too, are represented at Rosehill with inhabitants like **A.B. Dick** (1856-1934), originator of the duplicating machine; and **George S. Bangs** (1826-1877), designer of the railway mail car.

Deep within the cemetery, a small lake is ringed by prestigious family mausoleums housing the likes of railroad executive **Darius Miller**, whose interest in Egypt is visible in the stylings of his unique mausoleum; Vice-President **Charles Gates Dawes** (1865-1951), brigadier general and recipient of the Nobel Peace Prize; advertising mogul **Leo Burnett** (1891-1971); and the founding families of **Harris** Bank and **Goodrich** Tires. Near this charmed circle, the Horatio May Chapel stands sentinel, housing not only a beautifully ornate assembly room but also a holding vault, no longer used, for the storage of winter corpses until the spring thaw.

Just inside the Ravenswood Avenue gates, however, is the larger-than-life statue of **Charles Hull** (1820-1889), whose likeness keeps watch over the graves of his family. One of Chicago's pioneering residents, Hull gained fortune through real estate development, and fame when he leased his Halsted Street mansion to progressive activist Jane Addams. Hull House became the first of the nation's so-called settlement houses, a refuge of sorts for the homeless, friendless, poverty-stricken, and uneducated, where everyone from infants to the elderly could find shelter and food, learn language and other skills, indulge in sport, pursue the arts, and even study for citizenship tests. Addams's ultimate goal was to foster self-sufficiency in a time when the problems of urban life had begun to cause deep social and personal problems for city residents, especially immigrants.

Also deeply involved in the reform movement, and laid to rest not far from the Hull plot, is Evanstonian **Frances Willard** (1839-1898), founder of the Woman's Christian Temperance Union.

Towering near Willard's grave is the **Volunteer Fireman's Monument**, complete with a stone hose wrapped around a 36-foot marker. The first of such memorials in the United States, the 1864 masterpiece pays homage to the volunteer firefighters who died in the great South Water Street Fire of 1857. Renowned Lincoln sculptor **Leonard Volk** (1818-1895) designed the monument and went on to create a self-portrait in stone for placement on his own lot in Rosehill. Viewers of the Chicago-filmed *Backdraft* may recognize a replica of this monument; a "stunt double" was temporarily installed in *Graceland* Cemetery for the movie's purposes.

Arguably, the single most impressive cemetery experience to be had in the Chicago metropolitan area is the walk through the **Community Mausoleum** at Rosehill, the first ever large-scale communal crypt. Designed in 1914 by Sidney Lovell, the massive structure is a multi-level maze of marble-lined passageways stacked to the ceilings with thousands of dearly departed, including a number of notables from the world of retail—and Lovell himself.

In 1892, **Milton Florsheim** began making shoes in a small factory at Clinton and Adams streets. Though he focused on a high quality product from the beginning, believing that a fine shoe would sell better than a mediocre one, Florsheim knew that it would take more than a good product to make him a fortune. Investing in this belief, the entrepreneur sought out a number of potential retailers to set up shops across the country which would carry his footwear. While the shoemaker initially sold his product through small-town storefronts, he eventually branched out further, opening retail locations in the largest American cities; these were the first Florsheim shoe shops, which carried the entire line of Florsheim styles and sizes. Florsheim contin-

The front of Rosehill's community mausoleum, a severely classical building with a frieze depicting a Greek funeral scene (*above*). Immediately behind the center entrance is a colonnaded hallway modeled after the Parthenon leading to the John G. Shedd chapel. Behind the doorway on the right is the private room of Richard Warren Sears, founder of Sears, Roebuck and Company. (*Left*) Charles J. Hull, original owner of the Hull House made famous by Jane Addams.

The Volunteer Fireman's Monument by Leonard Volk (*right*). A self-portrait by sculptor Leonard Wells Volk (*below*), who also created numerous portraits of President Lincoln and Senator Stephen Douglas.

ued to use manufacturing and merchandising innovations to build up his trade, eventually creating a mammoth network of retailers that continues to operate today. His success earned him his hoped-for fortune, and, ultimately, a fitting place of repose among Chicago's other super salesmen.

Also here in the Community Mausoleum are merchandising arch-enemies, **Aaron Montgomery Ward** (1843-1913) and **Richard Warren Sears** (1863-1914), the latter of whom is said to walk the Mausoleum hallways, dressed to the nines in a topcoat and tails. Ghosts or not, illuminated only by the light leaking through the color-drenched panes of Louis Comfort Tiffany, the mausoleum is not for the faint-of-heart. The impressive surroundings, beautiful as they are, are dampened by both the clammy environment and the resulting, tell-tale scent of formaldehyde. Still, stiffen your lip and set your heart on getting a look at the most gloriously solemn burial site in the mausoleum: the family room of Aquarium namesake, **John G. Shedd** (1850-1926).

A New Hampshire native, Shedd migrated to Chicago in 1850, where he began a long and successful career with Marshall Field & Co., succeeding the department store's founder as company president in 1906. Though he achieved social and financial prominence through his work, Shedd guaranteed himself lasting fame when he spent $3 million on the development of what he dreamed would be the world's largest aquarium. Planned by a conscientious board of directors and built on landfill at the south end of Grant Park, the Shedd Aquarium was completed in 1929 and opened to 20,000 first-day visitors in May 1930.

One of the most intriguing and important aspects of the Aquarium was that it was the only inland aquarium to display both fresh- and saltwater varieties of aquatic life. The required sea water was transported via railroad cars, a million gallons at a time, from Key West, Florida. This practice continued on a regular basis for more than 40 years, until the Aquarium began simulating seawater in Chicago by a new process.

Though John G. Shedd died in 1926 (four years before his dream aquarium would open), the outstanding directors he had chosen for the project remained loyal to his specifications, contributing to Chicago and the world, and the memory of Shedd, one of the finest showcases of marine life in the world. A little piece of this paradise is silently reflected in the Shedd family room in Rosehill's Community Mausoleum. Before his death, the philanthropist commissioned a one-of-a-kind stained glass window from Tiffany that would bathe his crypt in blue light at sunset. The underwater theme of the family room is echoed in the skylit anteroom: even its chairs are adorned with the fanciful oceanic motifs of seahorses and shells.

The tallest monument in a Chicago Graveyard is the 70-foot obelisk of Mayor "Long John" Wentworth, who was 6'6" himself. Carved from a single piece of granite and erected in 1880, this obelisk cost the mayor $38,000.

Outside this labyrinth and far across the cemetery, claiming the largest lot in Rosehill, is former Chicago **Mayor "Long John" Wentworth** (1815-1888). The 6-foot, 6-inch Wentworth served several terms as a Democratic congressman before defecting to the Republican party, becoming an abolitionist and mayor of Chicago in the 1850s. A friend of President Abraham Lincoln, he was one of the honorary pall bearers when Lincoln's funeral train passed through Chicago. Hogging two-thirds of an acre of this vast burial ground, Wentworth also staked his claim with Rosehill's tallest monument: a 70-foot granite obelisk shooting to the north side skies. Accord-

Jumpin' that Train
Lincoln's Last, Long Haul

When the body of President Abraham Lincoln rolled into Chicago on its way to rest in Springfield, the city was waiting. Passing through a 40-foot high arch that had cost more than $15,000 to build, the coffin was removed from its rail car and carried through a countless sea of mourners for display. This spare-no-expense attitude had been reflected as well in the lavish preparations of Baltimore, Harrisburg, Philadelphia, New York, Albany, Buffalo, Cleveland, Columbus, and Indianapolis, each city striving to distinguish itself as the most gracious host of all.

Though the temporary surroundings varied, constant comfort was provided by the funeral car itself. Designed for Lincoln's use by the U.S. Military Railroad System, the car was run for the first time only after his death. Sadly, for the *United States* was the grandest example of railcar construction of its time, complete with 16 wheels, expertly crafted woodwork, etched-glass windows, and upholstered walls. In addition, its wheels were cleverly designed to allow undisrupted travel across the irregularly-spaced rails that remained for years after Lincoln himself signed legislation standardizing the gauge between rails. The president would surely have been tickled.

Even cities not on the funeral route did their best to impress the now-unimpressible president: the mayor of St. Louis, for example, provided the $6,000 hearse that awaited Lincoln in Springfield, festooned with lavish plumes and striking trim. And many towns along the route erected their own arches over the local railroad tracks in tribute. Perhaps most poignant was the one spanning the rails at Michigan City, Indiana, its epitaph gathering the sentiments of millions:

With Tears We Resign Thee to God and History;
The Purposes of the Almighty are Perfect and Must Prevail.

ing to the dictates of the deceased, no inscription was to be placed on the marker, so that the curious would ask whose it was; thus would he be assured a place at the center of conversation for years to come. Later, however, more sensible heads prevailed; the obelisk is now clearly inscribed with Wentworth's name and, for the uninformed, a list of his earthly achievements.

But don't ignore the lesser lights. At Rosehill, as at all cemeteries, every stone has its story, and a number of Chicago mayors have found more understated solace here at Rosehill: **George Bell Swift** (1845-1912), **Roswell Mason** (1805-1892), **Isaac Lawrence Milliken** (1815-1885), **DeWitt Clinton Cregier** (1829-1898), **John Roche** (1844-1904), **Levi Day Boone** (1808-1882), **John Blake Rice** (1809-1874), **Harvey Doolittle Colvin** (1815-1892), **Augustus Garrett** (1801-1848).

While the Windy City may have been driven by politics, it was made of meat and railroads, and students of its history will want to seek out the grave of local lunchtime hero **Oscar Mayer** (1859-1955), as well as the painstakingly detailed, miniature railway mail car which marks the grave of **George S. Bangs** (1826-1877), who designed the first of such transports. **George B. Armstrong** (d.1871), Chicago's assistant postmaster who founded the U.S. Railway Mail Service, reposes here as well.

Untimely deaths have brought many to Rosehill's soil, among them that of **Reinhart Schwimmer** (d. 1929), the unwitting eye doctor killed in the St. Valentine's Day Massacre.

Perhaps most poignant, however, is the grave of one of Chicago's most pitied homicide victims. In 1924, 14-year-old **Bobby Franks** was killed by two University of Chicago students, Nathan Leopold and Richard Loeb, who wanted to get some intel-

This remarkably lifelike railroad mail car honors its inventor, George S. Bangs. The car, tracks, and tunnel along with a more typical tree monument are carved in one piece of limestone.

"The Rock of Chicamauga," a granite boulder taken from that battlefield by the Grand Army of the Republic (*left*). Frances Pearce and her infant daughter, rendered in marble, lie within a glass box. This has been called the best cemetery monument in Chicago (*below*).

Rosehill's Romanesque Horatio N. May memorial chapel (*above*). (R*ight*) Major General Thomas E.G. Ransom, the "Phantom General" wounded in battle three times before being killed in battle in Georgia. Other Civil War soldiers are behind the general; their deteriorated markers having been recently replaced.

lectual kicks by committing the perfect crime. The ensuing kidnapping and murder of Franks led to the so-called Trial of the Century, during which the immortal Clarence Darrow successfully argued against the death penalty for Leopold and Loeb, though Loeb was later killed in prison by a fellow inmate.

After his demise, Bobby Franks was buried at Rosehill with the understanding that his lot number would not be given out to the curious. To this day, that information remains confidential; visitors can find the Franks grave among Rosehill's tens of thousands only by accident, or by a tip-off through the grapevine of local legend.

Almost as heart-wrenching as the murders of youth are the deaths of children taken by disease; the earth of 19th-century cemeteries is heavy with such casualties. Still, to the benefit of the modern observer, the unmatched grief of bereaved parents has inspired the commissioning of some of the most meticulous likenesses in funerary art, many of them so delicately detailed that they are encased under glass, such as the panes enclosing the Rosehill monument to young **Lulu Fellows**, who died at 16 in 1883. The beauty of the monument underscores the inscribed sentiment:

Many Hopes Lie Buried Here.

Another of Rosehill's glass-encased monuments has won wide artistic acclaim—the breathtaking sculpture of a reclining mother and child commissioned for the graves of **Frances Pearce** (d. 1864) and her infant daughter by grieving widower and father, Horatio Stone. The monument, designed by Chauncey Ives, was initially placed over the original pair of graves in the old City Cemetery. Upon the reinterment of the remains at Rosehill after City Cemetery closed, a protective glass encasement was added to protect the sculpture, which was named the Best Monument in Chicago by *Chicago Magazine*.

Yet with all of the accolades duly lavished on the residents of Rosehill, and their sumptuous memorials, perhaps no one grave here is currently more sought after than that of the city's beloved baseball broadcaster **Jack Brickhouse** (1916-1998).

ST. HENRY CEMETERY

Devon & Ridge Avenues
Chicago
773/561-2790
Catholic, Est. 1863

The towering church of St. Henry's, situated at Ridge and Devon avenues on the far north side, retains a decidedly old-fashioned character owing largely to its quaint adjacent churchyard. The original church and burial ground were established in the 1860s by Luxembourger settlers in the then-rural area. The current structure, erected in 1906, was designed by architect Henry J. Schlacks to serve German Catholics.

Today, most of the burials at St. Henry Cemetery involve Chicagoans of Hispanic origin, and the church itself has been claimed by Croatian worshipers and renamed Angel Guardian, in honor of the orphanage of the same name which once stood nearby. But traces of the site's heritage remain, namely in the surnames inscribed on older stones.

A nice addition to the cemetery is the **World War I Monument**, featuring an unusual sculpture of Christ comforting a soldier and sailor.

Celebrity hunters will find little satisfaction at this truly provincial site, though **Robert Ruekheim** (1913-1920)—the "Cracker Jack Boy"—and his uncle **Henry Muno** (1884-1958) do reside here.

Jesus comforts a soldier and sailor on St. Henry's World War I monument.

The Japanese Mausoleum, erected by the Japanese Mutual Aid Society, in the center of a carefully tended Japanese garden. The familiar rising sun motif appears on the front (*above*). Sarcophagi on the side porch of Montrose's chapel and crematorium building, about seven feet above the ground (*below*).

MONTROSE CEMETERY
5400 North Pulaski Road
Chicago
773/478-5400

In the early months of 1935, the Japanese Mutual Aid Society of Chicago formed to fulfill a very short and specific agenda: to purchase a substantial group of cemetery lots for Japanese-Americans, and to help with the burial fees for those who died unable to pay. The society chose Montrose Cemetery as their communal burial spot, and by 1937, a mausoleum had been completed at the site.

The formation of the society and the selection of the lots proved foresighted; with the rise of anti-Japanese sentiment during World War II came a proportional increase in rejection of Japanese-Americans by the established cemeteries. In addition, after the closing of the internment camps, more than 20,000 Japanese-Americans settled in the Chicago area; accordingly, the Japanese population at this cemetery also grew, forc-

Many cemeteries have monuments with an angel on the stairs leading up to a cross. This one, at Montrose, is one of the best. The scroll at the foot of the cross reads "God's Will, not ours, be done. Amen."

ing the expansion of the mausoleum as well as the purchase of lots surrounding the structure.

Montrose Cemetery also has a substantial Serbian-American section and plays host to an astounding array of ethnic populations, including Gypsies, East Indians, Iranians, Puerto Ricans, Mexicans, Cambodians, and others.

Pastor Gotthilf Lambrecht.

And those familiar with Chicago's history will be sobered by the **Iroquois Theatre Fire Memorial**. In December 1903, some 600 met their deaths in the brand-new, "absolutely fireproof" Iroquois, when a number of deadly circumstances, among them, exit doors that were either locked or that opened inward, combined to create the worst theater fire in U.S. history. Five years after the disaster, the Iroquois Memorial Association erected the unusual diamond-shaped monument that stands near the Montrose entrance gates. Today, the branches of a dead tree furnish a curious embellishment to the already striking memorial.

A distinct **crematorium and chapel building** in the classical style grace the grounds at Montrose: two side porticoes, about seven feet off the ground, have burials beneath the floors, each one covered with a ledger, or grave-length slab of stone.

BOHEMIAN NATIONAL CEMETERY
5255 North Pulaski Road
Chicago
773/478-0373
Est. 1877

Beginning in 1877, Bohemian National Cemetery attracted Czech settlers to Chicago's North Park neighborhood. Until that time, the area was occupied almost exclusively by German and Swedish immigrants who planted and harvested vegetables along the fertile shore of the North Branch of the Chicago River.

The cemetery itself began because of an incident in the Chicago Bohemian community in the years after the Great Fire. A woman named Marie Silhanek was denied burial at the available Catholic cemeteries, owing to the testimony of Fr. Joseph Molitor of St. James Church, who claimed Silhanek had not made a confession before death. The more than 25,000 members of the city's Bohemian population protested what they viewed as a

The entrance gate of Bohemian National Cemetery. The building features separate waiting rooms for men and women.

profound injustice, organizing against the authority of the Church to deny Christian burial to one of their own. By the late 1870s, the Bohemians had gathered enough support to found Bohemian National Cemetery, though the organization created for the task met with much protest from residents of Jefferson Township where the cemetery was to be located. The panicky population, imagining a replay of the disease and decay of the shuttered City Cemetery, urged the cemetery planners to abandon the project or find another site for its development.

Despite all pleas, and even a few unsuccessful lawsuits, Bohemian National Cemetery interred its first body in July of 1877.

Since its founding, the cemetery has hosted countless dedication ceremonies commemorating local, national, and international heroes and events. Such events have typically drawn enormous and enthusiastic crowds. Even on ordinary days, a number of points of interest continue to draw sightseers to Bohemian National.

For cemetery and funerary historians, the primary attraction here is the original funeral bell in the cemetery gate. The bell is the only one of such fixtures still remaining in Chicago; most others have been removed or replaced by modern substitutes.

One of the most popular destinations for non-mourners at Bohemian National is a sculpture by Albin Polasek commonly known as "The Grim Reaper"—a striking likeness of the foreboding figure, poised as if to en-

One of many
monuments
to victims of
the July 24,
1915 *Eastland*
disaster.

ter the **Stejskal-Buchal Family** mausoleum deep inside the cemetery.

Also of interest is Section 16, a communal plot occupied by many **victims of the 1915 *Eastland* Disaster**, in which the *Eastland* steamer, loaded to overflowing with Western Electric employees embarking on a picnic cruise from a downtown Chicago River dock, overturned, resulting in the deaths of more than 800 people, including 22 entire families.

Bohemian National is home to the mausoleum of the late **Mayor Anton Cermak** (1873-1933). Born near Prague in the 1870s, Cermak was raised as a Hussite: a follower of Protestant reformer John Huss. Immigrating to America when Anton was barely a year old, the Cermak family settled near 15th and Canal streets and later spent a number of years in the coal mining community of Braidwood far southwest of Chicago.

The mausoleum
of Mayor Anton
Cermak, shot
while making a
public appearance
with FDR.

It was only with the family's move back to the city, this time to a predominantly Bohemian west side neighborhood, that Anton began to see the value of a stable home base, especially in the pursuit of political life. The young Cermak made some attempts to succeed at business and soon found himself in the Illinois state legislature—for four terms. After serving those terms, Cermak was elected alderman, went on to serve as a court bailiff, and then returned to the post of alderman before being elected president of the Cook County Board of Commissioners in the early 1920s.

From the beginning, Cermak distinguished himself as a no-nonsense public figure; he was known to settle political debates by inviting opponents to "step outside," and he won many advocates by organizing the United Societies for Local Self-Government, which fought for the right of citizens to drink on Sunday. Leading the march against dry ordinances regulating liquor consumption, Cermak's alcoholic activism led the *Chicago Tribune* to label him "the wettest man in Chicago." Despite his bawdy style, however, Democratic Cermak went on to create the most organized political party the city had ever known. A prototype of efficiency, the party is credited as the first of its kind in the country to use statistical analysis in its strategic planning and performance evaluations.

Cermak's fatal mistake was sending police to rough up Frank Nitti, head of Chicago's most powerful mob. Assassin Giuseppe Zangara shot Cermak while he was on stage in Miami with President-elect Franklin D. Roosevelt. He lingered for a month after the shooting, then died after saying to Roosevelt, "I'm glad it was me instead of you." Cermak's legacy is well memorialized by his revered mausoleum at Bohemian National, which is inscribed with his famous words.

A draw not only for native Chicagoans, Bohemian patriots, too, will find a gold mine at this expansive site; monuments here commemorate some of the most moving events and influential personalities in Czech history.

A monument to **Ladimir Klacel** (1808-1882) was funded by donations from colleagues and admirers of the Bohemian philosopher. Expelled by the Austrian government in the 1860s on charges of radicalism, Klacel had been teaching at the Augustinian Friars School in Brno, Moravia, but was then forced to migrate to the United States. Here, he became a leading force in the Czech Rationalist movement until his death in 1882.

The **Lidice Memorial** keeps an eternal vigil to the victims of Adolph Hitler's 1942 attack on the tiny Czech town of Lidice. Staged in retaliation for the assassination of Reinhard Heydrich, Hitler's Chief of the Occupation forces in Czechoslovakia, by Czechoslovakian freedom fighters, the attack brought tanks and bulldozers rolling into the unsuspecting city, eliminating everything in their path. Simultaneously, women and children were evacuated from the city by force, many mothers separated forever from their offspring. Worst of all, the men of Lidice were gathered into a local barnyard and brutally mowed down by machine gun spray. Despite the gruesome display, Heydrich's assassins refused to surrender to Hitler. Amazingly, though one other village suffered a similar fate to that of Lidice, Nazi threats of further retaliation fizzled under the burden of overwhelming negative world opinion; the Bohemian dead became international heroes.

As the center of Czech nationalism in the United States, Chicago rocked with critical voices raging against the destruction of Lidice. A foundation was organized by *Chicago Sun-Times* publisher, Marshall Field, to raise money for a monument to the Lidice dead, and to re-name an American town after the vanquished Bohemian city. The plan reached speedy fruition: a small town outside of Joliet was chosen for erection of the monument and, upon its dedication, the town was re-christened Lidice. In Chicago, an urn of dirt from the destroyed Czech village was placed on display in the main chapel of the crematorium at Bohemian National Cemetery.

A second urn accompanies the Lidice memorial at Bohemian National, this one containing a mixture of soil and ashes from Poland's Osweiscim concentration camp, where hundreds of members of Czechoslovakian *sokols* (gymnastic societies) were executed.

Also greatly represented at Bohemian National are the contributions of Chicago Bohemians to American history. A **Civil**

Bohemian National's
Civil War memorial,
erected by the Grand
Army of the Republic
(*left*). The chapel and
crematorium building,
which also houses BNC's
columbarium sections.
The bronze statue in
front is *Mother* by
Albin Polasek (*below*).

An American flag holds the place of honor inside BNC's chapel, which was prominently featured in the recent film *U.S. Marshals* (*above*). A Spanish-American War monument, dedicated 1926 (*right*).

War Veterans Monument was dedicated here in 1889 with much fanfare; more than 100 testimonials, contributed by numerous Czech organizations, were sealed in the marker's cornerstone.

Another patriotic structure is the **United Spanish War Veterans Memorial**, popularly known as "The Hiker Monument" for its sculpture of an American soldier in Spanish-American War battle gear. The soldier's hulking pedestal is a solid piece of granite, which was transported to Bohemian National from Wausau, Wisconsin. Dedicated in 1926, the entire monument was erected by the Bohemian American Camp No. 30, United Spanish War Veterans.

A fine tradition perseveres at the **World War I and II Memorial**. An American flag has been flown from the monument's flagpole since the memorial's dedication in 1952, but these banners are frequently changed. Over the years, hundreds of veterans' families have donated flags to be flown over the site in honor of their deceased loved ones.

By far the most spectacular feature at Bohemian National is its **indoor columbarium**. Columbariums are walls with niches for the storage of urns of human ashes. In most cemeteries, these niches are enclosed with front panels of granite or marble that are decorated with a simple name plate. Here, the columbariums have frames of iron and bronze, with front panels of glass that allow the contents to be seen. Urns range from elaborately carved wooden

After the Fire
The Trouble with Cremains

With a cost of less than half that of embalming, increasing numbers are choosing the fiery furnace as their postmortem destination. In the United States, cremation is now preferred by 20 percent of the year's dead, up from a scant four percent in the 1950s, and that figure is expected to reach nearly 50 percent in the next ten years.

Appropriately, the Cremation Society of North America is evangelizing against the "ignorance" of Americans who insist on calling that shoe box full of somebody, "ashes." Indeed political correctness shakes its finger even in the crematorium: the proper term is "cremains," thank you very much.

In fact, the fruit of the inferno is not dust but fragments, the knobby, gnarled, and broken bones left behind after the literal vaporization, at 1,800 degrees, of everything else. It is the pulverization of these cremains that yields the powdery substance of popular imagination.

Whether gathered together *au naturel* or ground to smithereens, cremains are indeed remains and, as such, they must *go* somewhere. A coffin is still the most prevalent container, though the urn is commonly thought to be the most logical.

For those who do choose the urn, the decision making has just begun. A plastic repository may be purchased for about $20. If your budget is a little bigger, the 24K-gold-plated, sapphire-studded ones are $3,500.

What to do with this conversation piece? Bequeath it to your beloved or buy a nook in a columbarium, where you'll reside for eternity within a proper mausoleum.

If these choices are too tiresome, forego them. Scatter yourself instead. If, however, you choose as your burial site a piece of public land, a site in a national park, a river, lake, or beach, don't tell anyone about your plans; most statutes call it littering. For while cremains are perfectly healthy, the idea of them still makes most constituents' skin crawl.

If the urn seems too cramped, and scattering too criminal, there is one other legal option. For less than $5,000, Houston-based Celestis, Inc. will happily shoot your "ashes" into outer space. There, they are promised to orbit the Earth for several years—before exploding in a blaze of glory.

boxes to cardboard cylinders marked "temporary container." Most niches are highly decorated and personalized, filled with photographs, artificial flowers, flags, and, in one case, a miniature mausoleum of white marble. The eternal residents of the BNC Columbarium exude personality at a fraction of the cost of traditional stone monuments.

At least one final monument deserves commentary: that dedicated simply and powerfully to *Mother*. Designed by Albin Polasek, the monument was erected in commemoration of the cemetery's 50th anniversary and dedicated before a reported audience of 25,000 people. A stirring tribute to an unmatched profession, the memorial's sculpture of a woman sheltering her children continues to be a favorite with visitors from around the world.

BETH-EL CEMETERY
5736 North Pulaski Road
Chicago
Jewish, Est. late 1800s

RIDGELAWN CEMETERY
5736 North Pulaski Road
Chicago
Jewish, Est. late 1800s

Across the road from Bohemian National, just north of Montrose Cemetery on Pulaski Road, are two diminutive Jewish cemeteries dating to the late 19th century. Visitors quickly discover that all of the headstones face symbolically eastward.

For those not visiting loved ones, a popular destination at Beth-El is the stirring **Eichenbaum Monument** near the front entrance, comprised of a sturdy base supporting the likeness of a dying lion.

METRO NORTH

Contrast these modern gates at Des Plaines's All Saints Cemetery with
the original entranceway seen in the photo on page 77.

Colonel James Mulligan commanded Chicago's "Irish Brigade"
in the Civil War. He was killed in battle in the Shenandoah Valley
in 1864. Mulligan's monument is prominently located near
Calvary cemetery's main entrance.

CALVARY CEMETERY

301 Chicago Avenue
Evanston
847/864-3050
Catholic, Est. 1859

As more and more individuals and congregations were high-
tailing it out of the Chicago City Cemetery, the Roman Catholic
Diocese saw fit to follow the lead. A parcel of land in the town of
Evanston, just north of Chicago along the Lake Michigan shoreline, had been purchased by the Diocese in the 1850s, and the
site was slated as a suitable one for communal burial. Consecra-
tion took place in 1859, and the gates of Calvary were opened to
re-interment of the faithful from City Cemetery, as well as
numbers of newly-departed church members, many of them of
Irish descent.

The ethnic origins of the bereaved are revealed in many ways
here, especially by the many crucifixes and stone firemen's
helmets adorning various gravesites. In addition, Roman Catholic shrines dot the expanse, as well as monuments marking the
gatherings of various religious orders. Near the gorgeous gate,
designed by James Egan to resemble the Greek letters *alpha* and
omega (Catholic symbols of the everlasting God), a **Priest's
Circle** serves as a final resting place for the cemetery's numerous ordained residents, their stones identified with chalices and
other motifs.

Nearby is the stone tribute to Civil War hero **Colonel
Mulligan** (d. 1864), commander of the "Irish Brigade."

Squeezed in between the winding lakefront stretch of
Sheridan Road on the east and Evanston's Chicago Avenue (the
extension of North Clark Street) on the west, Calvary shelters a
number of popular local heroes (and villains), including **Lawrence Kelly** (d. 1974), co-founder of Chicago Lyric Opera;
Edward Hines, lumber giant; and meat packer **John Cudahy** (d.
1915). Several of the city's mayors join them, including **Edward**

One of Chicagoland's many poignant graveyard monuments of children, this one has brothers Artie and Willie Walsh looking east toward a modern shrine, their soft marble features nearly worn away (*above*). Dedicated to "Mother," one of Calvary's old mausoleums (*below*).

F. Dunne (1853-1937), **Edward Kelly** (1876-1950), **Martin Kennelley** (1887-1961), and **John P. Hopkins** (1858-1918).

Also here at Calvary is **Charles Comiskey** (1859-1931), owner of the 1919 Chicago Black Sox. By the age of 17, the Chicago native was playing professional baseball and by his mid-20s managing the St. Louis Browns. After a number of years of playing for and managing several teams, Comiskey emerged as owner and president of the Chicago White Sox. After working to organize the American League, he brought his team into its ranks and stuck with the Chicago club for 30 years until his death, at which time he was succeeded by his son Louis.

Calvary's other baseball monument features crossed bats and honors **"Everybody's friend, Little Bob Figg"** (1872-1926).

John M. Smyth (d. 1909), furniture salesman, is also buried in Calvary, leaving behind an empire of Homemakers retail stores.

And here lies crooked politician extraordinaire, **Michael "Hinky Dink" Kenna** (1857-1946), alderman of the legendarily corrupt First Ward, who once ruled the notorious Levee with partner-in-slime "Bathhouse" John Coughlin. Lauded by prostitutes, gamblers, bootleggers, and police chiefs, the "Lords of the Levee" held no prejudices: they took bribes and gave them with wild abandon, assembling a constituency comprised of everyone from madams to mayors. The will of the 89-year-old Kenna included a provision for a $33,000 mausoleum, aside from the $1 million bequeathed to his family. Kenna's heirs had other plans; namely, an $85 headstone reading

MICHAEL KENNA
1857-1946

Joining Kenna at Calvary are the far more innocent **Artie and Willie**, brothers who died at the ages of four and two. Huddling together in a grotto-like niche, the pair once looked over a miniature lagoon, since replaced by the cemetery's shrine to St. Peter. The marble features of the two boys are almost completely worn away by a century of weathering. Another statue of a child is better preserved—a sculpted likeness of **Josie Lyons** (d. 1891) stands inside a hollow stone cylinder, protected by a glass door that allows viewing.

Calvary also shelters beloved author **James T. Farrell** (1904-1979), famous for his semi-autobiographical fiction chronicling life in Chicago's Irish Catholic neighborhoods. Farrell's perceptive accounts of the city's southeast side experience won him countless fans, especially with the publication of his epic trilogy, *Studs Lonigan*.

And storytellers will delight in Calvary's haunting legend which tells of a World War II aviator, reported to have drowned off the rocky Lake Michigan shore during a training flight. For decades the phantom of this hapless young man was reported to drag himself out of the water and across Sheridan Road, disappearing through the cemetery gates. To date, he has not been identified with any particular Calvary burial, and sightings seem to have ceased sometime during the 1960s.

John A. Lynch and family have a small section at Calvary entirely to themselves, bounded by low stone coping.

CHURCH OF THE HOLY COMFORTER
222 Kenilworth Avenue
Kenilworth
847/251-6120
Protestant

Visitors making the trek to Calvary may continue further up the shore to the posh community of Kenilworth, where journalist and poet **Eugene Field** (1850-1895) rests in the courtyard of this community landmark.

FORT SHERIDAN CEMETERY
Fort Sheridan
East of Sheridan Road
Highwood

Situated just north of the Cook County border, this richly historic site nonetheless deserves inclusion in Chicago's cemetery inventory.

Officially abandoned and under residential development, the National Historic District of Fort Sheridan continues to draw a steady stream of visitors to its impressive surroundings studded with the architecture of Holabird & Roche. The main attractions at the lakefront complex continue to be of the artistic and architectural variety: namely, the looming 150-foot water tower and a glorious monument portraying fort namesake Philip Sheridan. Following closely in popularity is the fort's cemetery, which provides everlasting refuge for **Phillipp Spinner**, **August Siefert**, and **John Hackett**, all of whom rode with Custer at Little Bighorn.

MEMORIAL PARK CEMETERY
9900 Gross Point Road
Skokie
773/583-5080

Chicagoans will remember the murder of **Karyn "Cookie" Kupcinet** (1941-1963), daughter of longtime Chicago columnist, Irv. Cookie was interred here upon her untimely death in 1963.

But this 20th-century Skokie cemetery is better known for another of its celebrities: **Robert Reed** (1932-1992), otherwise known as a man named Brady. The Highland Park native became famous to families across the country as Mr. Mike Brady of television's popular sitcom, *The Brady Bunch* (1969-1974).

Also at rest here is former American League President, **Will Harridge** (1883-1971), as well as football Hall of Famer, **Sid Luckman** (1916-1998), whose star quarterbacking led the Chicago Bears to four National Football League championships in the 1940s.

And those unimpressed by popular culture may yet appreciate the cemetery's Gothic crematorium and chapel.

This old community mausoleum is in the western half of St. Adalbert's.

ST. ADALBERT CEMETERY
6800 North Milwaukee Avenue
Niles
847/647-9845
Catholic, Est. 1872

By the last decade of the 19th century, five predominantly Polish neighborhoods had been established in Chicago, each in heavily industrialized areas: the Lower West Side, sheltering workers in the factories along the ship canal and the Burlington Railroad, the steel mill-centered community of South Chicago; Back-of-the-Yards on the southwest side, and the Polish Downtown area just west of Goose Island. The latter of these was more than 85 percent Polish in 1898; in one precinct, the percentage actually reached 99.9, with only one non-Pole counted among its 2,500 residents. The churches in this area served more than 24,000 Polish immigrants and included two of the largest Roman Catholic communities in the world: St. Stanislaw Kostka and Holy Trinity.

Several monuments at St. Adalbert's portray the Holy Family: Jesus, the Virgin Mary, and St. Joseph.

Along with worship, one of the main bases for community establishment for Poles as well as other ethnic groups was the problem of death. Chicago's immigrants were understandably haunted by the prospect of dying far from their homeland, and the desperate desire to rest in peace prompted the formation of

A row of tree-shaded mausoleums at St. Adalbert's resembles
a city street (*above*). A low border of granite encloses this plot
at St. Adalbert's Cemetery (*below*). The upright monument in the
rear is one of the most popular styles found in Catholic cemeteries
of the early 20th century. Another noteworthy element of this site
is its ledger, a full-length flat grave cover.

This bronze and granite World War I memorial stands near the main office of St. Adalbert's.

mutual aid societies. For the city's Polish workers, these societies aimed primarily to provide widows with the burial fees needed upon the deaths of their blue-collar husbands. To this end, St. Adalbert Cemetery, perhaps the largest Polish cemetery in the metropolitan area, was established in nearby Niles in 1872. A modest site at first, the acreage grew tremendously as Polish and Bohemian parishes bought increasingly large portions of land to sell to their parishioners.

The majority of contemporary visitors to St. Adalbert's travel clear across the huge expanse from the Milwaukee Avenue gates to reach the newer section beyond the access road. A profusion of flowers and wreaths, fresh and artificial, flower boxes marked with peel-and-stick letters identifying the surnames of the dead, candles, musical greeting cards, toys and other offerings covers the gently sloping area, and the entire modern section is overseen by the **Shrine to St. Maximillian Kolbe** (1894-1941), memorializing the Polish-born Franciscan friar, publisher, and missionary imprisoned in Auschwitz in 1941. While so confined, Father Kolbe begged his captors to take his own life in exchange for the life of another prisoner. They agreed, and Kolbe was slated for starvation. When his body neglected to give up after several weeks, officials became impatient, and the prisoner was given a lethal dose of carbolic acid, which Kolbe is remembered to have received cheerfully. His body was cremated, fulfilling his wish to use himself "completely up in the service of the Immaculata." Kolbe was canonized in 1982, not long before Chicago compatriots erected the local shrine to his memory.

Other notables buried here are **Fredrak Fraske** (1874-1973), the last surviving veteran of the Indian Wars, and football icon and local hero **George "Papa Bear" Halas** (1895-1983).

Inseparable from St. Adalbert Cemetery is Przyblo's House of the White Eagle, a banquet hall which stands across the street from the cemetery gates on Milwaukee Avenue. Built on an old Polish picnic ground, Przyblo's plays host to hundreds of funeral parties each year, mourners pouring in to feast and drink after graveside services.

Monuments in the shape of dead trees are quite common in Chicagoland graveyards, but usually stand alone. Here, two trees encircled with an intricate vine form an arch, supporting a cross between them.

50 (Thousand) Ways to Leave Your Loved Ones
Burial Customs To Die For

Perhaps nothing says more about a person, or a culture, than funerary desires. From ancient pyres to electric crematoriums, from interment—whether underground burial, in a tomb, or in an urn—to burial at sea and the scattering of ashes, an individual may wish to be laid to rest with a cherished chihuahua, in a glass coffin, seated behind the wheel of a beloved racing car, or lowered into a grave filled with rosebuds.

Though such whims run high on the list of influences, ethnicity and religion have always been the most common and uncompromising arbiters of burial arrangements. Consider, for example, the Medieval Chinese emperors who, upon their passing, took along their cookpots, as well as their soldiers and horses, to make the afterworld as homey as possible. Then there are the modern Indian Parsis who carry their corpses to a so-called tower of silence, where they are left to be eaten by carrion birds. The Bishnoi of Rajasthan dump their dead in unmarked trenches, covering the bodies with salt. Most Hindu Indians, however, are simply cremated according to religious dictates, and for a price of about $12.

Climate also has its say. Bereaved Russians may well leave their unembalmed beloved overnight in a chilly church to await the next day's funeral party. But the suffocating Pakistani heat insists on same-day services, even if relatives are away. And Americans are well-acquainted with the New Orleans practice of above-ground burial in whitewashed "high rise" tombs, owing to bad memories of heavy rains.

Cost, too, is forever a consideration. In China, one may take leave of this world for $50; in Japan, mourners might be allowed a few more tears, stuck as they often are with a funeral bill of nearly $32,000.

In industrialized countries, considerations become increasingly contemporary. In Britain, where 400,000 of the regions 640,000 yearly dead are cremated, environmental activists are up in arms over the burning of so many wooden caskets. Thus the birth of the Natural Death Centre, which offers burial in a cardboard casket as part of its "Green Funeral" plan. After burial, the plot is identified not by a headstone, but with a newly-planted tree.

Whether cardboard or 24-karat, the casket remains, in modernized nations, the most popular destination for embalmed corpses as well as ashes. Traditional graves or tombs, preceded by formal services, continue to be chosen by the great majority of funeral planners. In the positivistic intellectual climate of the West, it is perhaps surprising that millions consider the resultant "cost of dying," in the U.S. $3,000 to $5,000 on average, a necessary expense. Yet, the carved and gilded casket, the lavish embalming services, one or two days of display at the local funeral home, and a custom marker over a scenic plot all continue to be touted, and ultimately included, as key components of a "proper" burial.

Though burial customs are among the slowest of all traditions to change, a shift might at last be coming. While the funeral industry is presently booming, their custom caskets and state-of-the-art embalming equipment may soon be gathering dust, as increasing numbers of would-be customers confess to a nagging feeling that the rituals propagated by the modern mortician are nothing short of morbid.

SUNSET MEMORIAL PARK
3100 Shermer Road
Northbrook
847/724-0669

This Northbrook site was opened for North Shore blacks, excluded from the white cemeteries by increasing Jim Crow attitudes and geographically from the new black cemeteries located in the far southern reaches of Cook County.

ALL SAINTS CEMETERY
700 North River Road
Des Plaines
847/298-0450
Catholic, Est. 1923

Not to be confused with its decidedly Polish, city cousin on Higgins Road, this Des Plaines site is Irish in origin, though currently home to many ethnic groups.

The still-burgeoning burial ground recently rippled with sensationalism when it opened its gates for the burial of "nanny" victim, **Matthew Eappen** (d. 1997, age 8 months). But cheerier visits are also to be made here. Along with thousands of common folk, All Saints provides eternal homes to **George Halas, Jr.** (1925-1979), Son of "Papa Bear"; professional wrestler **Walter Palmer** (1912-1998); and baseball Hall of Famer, Cubs catcher **Charles "Gabby" Hartnett** (1900-1972). Yet it is another sports immortal that lately draws so many visitors to this sprawling

ossuary. Since his death in 1998, **Harry Caray** (1914-1998), the beloved broadcaster of the Chicago Cubs, has rendered the confines of this cemetery decidedly friendlier.

With his signature glasses, unmistakable voice, and unswervable enthusiasm, Caray made the baseball game a quintessentially Chicago experience with his famed Seventh Inning Stretch, in which he led a daily crop of die-hards in "Take Me Out to the Ball Game." A year after his death, celebrity guests continue the charismatic Caray's tradition, offering their own varyingly vitriolic versions of the classic tune.

SHALOM MEMORIAL PARK
1700 West Rand Road
Arlington Heights
847/255-3520
Jewish

This Arlington Heights site boasts one of the largest Holocaust memorials in the Midwest: The **Tower of Remembrance**, stretching to an imposing 80 feet.

II. WEST

The agonized Christ sculpted as part of this tree monument
can be seen at All Saints Polish National Catholic Cemetery.

CITY WEST

A cross made of pipes at St. Nicholas Ukrainian Cemetery.

Like most other Catholic cemeteries, All Saints Polish National Catholic features several "tree" monuments. This one is more elaborate than most: it features an angel with a crucifix, and a nest of birds and a squirrel carved above the three inset portraits.

ALL SAINTS POLISH NATIONAL CATHOLIC CEMETERY

9201 West Higgins Road
Chicago
773/380-7131
Polish National Catholic

This Higgins Road burial ground was established to serve Chicago-area followers of the so-called Polish National Catholic Church. Since the beginning of Polish immigration to the United

A close-up view of the ample gravemarker for Anthony Kozlowski, bishop and founder of the Polish National Catholic Church.

States, transplanted Poles had found fault with the American administration of the Roman Catholic Church, believing that its authority was overwhelmingly centered in Irish leaders. In Chicago, Fr. Anthony Kozlowski took it upon himself to establish the Church of All Saints to serve potential congregants who felt disenfranchised by the established parish communities. For his efforts, Kozlowski was excommunicated by Archbishop Feehan, but the renegade priest forged on, founding the Polish Old Catholic Church and winning a devoted legion of followers. Visitors to All Saints Polish National Catholic should note that this is the only Chicago cemetery with its own picnic area, providing for the ethnic custom of picnicking at the graves of loved ones.

SAINT NICHOLAS UKRAINIAN CEMETERY

8901 West Higgins Road
Chicago
773/693-9718

This congregational cemetery contains nationals from the entire metropolitan area, who rest beneath gravemarkers emblazoned with suns and inscribed with both native and English epitaphs. Monuments here are highly individual and colorful; they include such things as crosses made from pipe and grave covers of brick amidst the more common granite stones.

A bishop rests beneath this black granite sarcophagus, guarded by both the American and Ukrainian flags. Behind him are several rows of priests with identical monuments.

With its colorful (red, blue, gold, and white) depiction of Madonna and Child, this family headstone is typical of the colorfulness and religious imagery seen at St. Nicholas Cemetery.

ST. JOHN'S/ST. JOHANNES CEMETERY
O'Hare International Airport
Chicago
Protestant, Est. 1837

REST HAVEN CEMETERY
O'Hare International Airport
Chicago

Before the age of air travel, these two farmland cemeteries existed where O'Hare International Airport now sprawls. The founding date of St. Johannes, 1837, matches that of southwest suburban St. James-Sag, seeming to tie the two as the oldest Chicago-area cemeteries. Yet, burials at St. James-Sag are assumed to have taken place before that cemetery's official founding, and so St. Johannes remains an unrecognized secret.

Until the 1950s, residents of this rural area enjoyed quiet visits to their local cemeteries, the nearby Orchard Place Airport

This white marble monument at St. John's is so worn,
the writing is barely legible.

generally minding its own business. When the city took over the airport, however, officials annexed the land around it, re-naming the field in honor of Chicago World War II veteran, Edward O'Hare. The annexed land included the two cemeteries, which soon became decidedly unrestful, but great for plane spotters. Would-be visitors can access the grounds by driving in from Irving Park Road.

A wistful sight at Rest Haven is the ruined monument over the grave of three-year-old **Laura Elfring** (1895-1898). The now decapitated statue depicts a young girl holding a dove in her left hand. Also especially poignant is the round stone remembering the mere six days of life given to little **Emma Luehring** (May 11, 1903-May 17, 1903).

Keep a lookout for air traffic when you're heading for St. Johannes; the cemetery is nestled between an east-west runway and the Federal Express hangar. Originally the churchyard for a congregation since relocated to the suburb of Bensenville, St. Johannes, otherwise known as St. John's, remains a well-pre-

Henry Kolze's obelisk, the tallest monument at St. Johannes, on the grounds of O'Hare Airport.

served example of an old German Protestant cemetery. Visitors are usually drawn here because of the churchyard's unique setting, but a pair of sites are worth searching for: the monument to St. John's **Pastor William Boerner** and a row of four lectern-shaped markers dating to the 1890s. Also of interest is a large wooden cross at the north end of the cemetery, a 20th-century addition marking the spot where the church once stood.

COOK COUNTY POOR FARM AND INSANE ASYLUM

Irving Park Road & Narragansett Avenue
Chicago

From 1851 through 1910, an expanse of land at Irving Park Road and Narragansett Avenue in the then-suburb of Dunning was utilized by the county as a hospital, tuberculosis sanitarium, insane asylum, and cemetery complex.

Several years before the closing of the complex, the medical facilities were moved to the town of Oak Forest, and in 1912 the state purchased the land from Cook County for $1. Though burials at the site continued until the early 1920s, many of the records were lost. Eventually, the cemetery was abandoned, and the potter's field, containing an estimated 38,000 deceased, went to weed.

Only in recent years were the site's remains unearthed, during the break-up of land for the building of Wright College, the Ridgemoor Estates residences, and a shopping complex called Dunning Square.

Plans to create a memorial park on the site have been slow-moving, greatly due to the difficulty in re-seeding the property. Upon the completion of landscaping, the proposed expanse, 66,000 square feet worth, will host the re-interment of excavated remains, now in storage, and the new burials at Read-Dunning Memorial Park will be identified by historical indicators representing the deceased.

ROBINSON WOODS INDIAN BURIAL GROUND
Robinson Woods North
Lawrence Avenue & East River Road
Chicago

T he **Robinson Family graves** are located in Robinson Woods North, part of the Forest Preserve District of Cook County's far northwest side holdings. Named for Alexander Robinson—Chief Che-Che-Pin-Quay—leader of the Potawatomi, Ottawa, and Chippewa tribes, the burial ground is easily accessed by pulling into the site's own wayside at Lawrence Avenue and East River Road and is subject to the same visitation rules as other FPD property.

At the Treaty of Prairie du Chien, Robinson, an important Chicago settler who greatly enhanced relations between the native and early white residents of the city, was awarded a large segment of land and an annuity for his role in the negotiations. The burial ground is part of that land, where Robinson's descendants lived until the mid-20th century.

Today, the site survives as a tiny clearing at the threshold of this popular preserve.

The Robinson graves are marked by a large boulder bearing a memorial inscription, and visitors may rest on nearby stone benches before beginning a hike or bike through the woods.

WESTLAWN CEMETERY
7801 West Montrose Avenue
Chicago
773/625-8600
Jewish

During the second influx of Jews to Chicago during the latter half of the 19th century, Jewish cemeteries were characterized by a strict sectionalization of groups, according to membership in various synagogues, fraternities, *Vereins* (societies), or *Landsmanschaften* (compatriot associations). By the 1920s, however, newly-founded burial grounds were following the lead of patrons of non-Jewish cemeteries, who were opting for individual or family plots over communal burial with their spiritual or secular organizations. Westlawn is a good example of this shift in practice; the amply-spaced, individual markers are typically grouped with those of other family members, and the majority of inscriptions are in English.

A number of luminaries of the entertainment industry repose at Westlawn, including some unique contributors to American culture.

In 1924, Chicago's Savoy Ballroom at South Park and Kedzie avenues had fallen on hard times, and in order to draw better crowds, the hall's owners began holding basketball games before the dances. Twenty-four-year-old **Abe Saperstein** (1902-1966) begged the Savoy to sponsor his new team; when they did, he dubbed it the "Savoy Big Five." The idea flopped, but the team wanted to stay together, and Saperstein took them on the road in his Model T Ford. The team consisted of Tommy Brookings, William Grant, Lester Johnson, Walter Wright, Inman Jackson, Joe Lillard, William Watson, and Randolph Ramsey, and they made their debut on January 7, 1927, in Hinckley, Illinois, sporting hand-me-down jerseys emblazoned with "New York." Later, Saperstein added two more words to the jersey, and a sensation was born: "Saperstein's New York Globetrotters." The rest, as they say, is history.

Joining Saperstein at Westlawn is quintessential movie reviewer **Gene Siskel** (1946-1999). Falling victim to complications from a brain tumor, the Chicago-bred personality died in early 1999, leaving behind a legion of filmgoers, who are left to turn to partner in criticism, Roger Ebert, for reel-time recommendations. Siskel was raised by his aunt and uncle after his parents died when he was nine years old. Attending Yale University, the enthusiastic Gene got a job with the *Chicago Tribune* two years after his graduation in 1967. In the mid-1970s, Siskel joined forces with Ebert to create the local public television movie-review program, *Sneak Previews*. After seven years, the pair sold their concept into syndication when their locally-popular banter clicked with national audiences. Carried along by Siskel and Ebert's good-natured competitive criticism, the show went on to become a major influence on box-office draws during the '80s and '90s.

Nightclub owner **Jack Ruby** (1911-1967) finally eluded the press here at Westlawn. Ruby was born and buried in Chicago; in between, he ran numbers for Al Capone's crowd and assassinated Lee Harvey Oswald.

And, playing for the other side on the other side: Westlawn resident **Albert N. "Wallpaper" Wolff** (1903-1998), one of Eliott Ness's legendary crew, whose gravemarker identifies him as *Last of the FBI Untouchables*.

ACACIA PARK CEMETERY

7800 West Irving Park Road
Chicago
773/625-7800
Masonic

South of Westlawn is Acacia Park, a cemetery founded by Freemasons. Two obelisks decorated with Masonic symbols stand atop small hills in tribute to these origins. As all grave-markers here are uniform in size, Acacia Park's most remarkable structure aside from these obelisks is its large **community mausoleum**, which features a Masonic chapel and several private rooms as spectacular as those found in Rosehill's Community Mausoleum. At the very top of the mausoleum is a long, narrow room accessible only by an ancient elevator; among those entombed here is **Alvah Roebuck** (1864-1948), business partner of Richard Sears.

A statue of a woman leaning sorrowfully on a broken pillar stands at the base of one of Acacia Park's obelisks.

One of a pair of obelisks, the dominant features at Acacia Park that are visible from Irving Park Road. The monument is marked with the Masonic square and compass.

Together Forever
The Many Ties That Bind

The impetus towards group identification is not limited to this life. In fact, perhaps nowhere is the insistence on "set-apartedness" more obvious than in the modern cemetery.

In Chicago, as elsewhere, religious differences demanded the first divisions, when Catholics and Protestants insisted on separate burial grounds during the establishment of the earliest municipal cemeteries. After the closing of these graveyards and the opening of new Catholic, Protestant, and non-sectarian sites, ethnic prejudice began to emerge; German Catholics, for example, shuddered at the Irish overtones of the Diocesan cemetery, Calvary, opting instead to establish the burial ground of St. Boniface as bluntly Germanic. And even within these exclusive enclosures segregation continued, the dead being clustered according to membership in military organizations, singing societies, and other groups. Jewish cemeteries, too, were obsessed with division, erecting rigid gated fences between the sections owned by differing congregations and social groups.

In the so-called "non-sectarian" cemeteries of Graceland, Rosehill, and Oak Woods, among others, another kind of self-sorting is evident: the class structure of late 19th- and early 20th-century

Exterior and interior views of the impressive Acacia Mausoleum, eternal home of Sears partner Alvah Roebuck.

Chicago could be easily mapped today by simply noting the names of those buried in the posh central sections, encrusted with marble, lavishly landscaped, and refreshed with pools and lakes, and those recorded on the modest markers and closely-crowded flush stones skirting the grounds.

Obvious, too, is the everlasting bond of brotherhood, made tangible at death by the erection of common monuments by the Freemasons, the Eastern Star, the Woodmen, the Elks, the Odd Fellows, the Rebekah Lodge, and other fraternities and sister organizations.

Careers, too, often set graves apart; modern cemeteries are often rife with group burials of military divisions, police and fire personnel, members of religious orders, railroad workers, and even waiters and bartenders. In west suburban Woodlawn Cemetery, a large section dubbed "Showmen's Rest" is set aside for the burial of circus performers.

Sadly, but because misery loves company, victims of tragedies are sometimes gathered together as well. Witness, for example, the heart-wrenching local memorials to the Iroquois Theatre fire, the capsizing of the *Eastland* steamer, and the devastating conflagration at Our Lady of the Angels parish school, among too many others. And the new children's sections at many burial grounds—rich with gifts of toys, candy, balloons, and comic books—attest to the particularly poignant commonality of their silent residents.

IRVING PARK CEMETERY
7777 West Irving Park Road
Chicago
773/625-3500

Brothers-with-arms **Frank** (d. 1929) **and Peter** (d. 1929) **Gusenberg** were buried at this Chicago cemetery after being fatally tommy-gunned in the St. Valentine's Day Massacre. As members of the O'Banion/Weiss/Moran North Side gang, the brothers were a tough pair. In fact, Frank actually lived through the massacre, surviving long enough to make it to the hospital. Riddled with machine gun fire and utterly doomed, he was questioned there by police about the identity of the assailants. But Gusenberg refused to rat. In answer to the pleas of desperate detectives for an identification, Frank replied simply and scowlingly, "I ain't no copper." They would be his last words.

Mount Olive Cemetery's entrance gate on Narragansett Avenue.

MOUNT OLIVE CEMETERY
3800 North Narragansett Avenue
Chicago
773/286-3770

Claiming the largest section of an impressive cemetery complex, Mt. Olive shares a piece of Chicago with Mt. Mayriv, Mt. Isaiah, Mount B'nai B'rith, and Rosemont Park. Rosemont Park is noted for its unusual topiary-studded landscape and as the final resting place of boxer **David Barney Ross** (1909-1967).

This striking Scandinavian water fountain near the entrance is a reminder of the ancestry of many of those buried in Mount Olive Cemetery.

Strollers in late-19th century Mt. Olive will come upon the obsolete railroad grade which once served trains traveling to and from the old Cook County Poor Farm and Insane Asylum, located until 1910 near the area now known as Dunning Square.

Originally founded for Chicago's Scandinavians, as evidenced by the delightful Viking drinking fountain near the entry arch, the cemetery has more recently hosted the burials of Latvians, Armenians, and other ethnic groups.

While there is no shortage of mourners here, an extremely uncommon glass mausoleum draws many cemetery buffs as well to this eclectic site.

METRO WEST

Graves in a central section of Jewish Waldheim Cemetery.

ST. JOSEPH CEMETERY
Belmont & Cumberland Avenues
River Grove
708/453-0184
Catholic

Even ultra-slippery gangster **Lester Gillis** (1908-1934), a.k.a. "Baby Face" Nelson, couldn't run from the reaper. He is buried at this River Grove site.

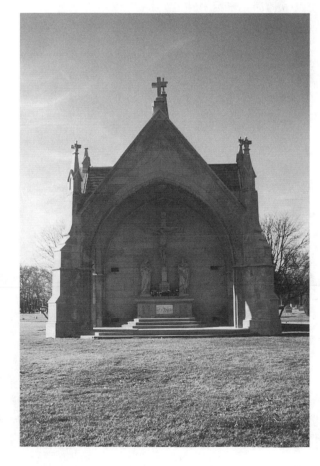

An open-air chapel at St. Joseph's Cemetery.

This monument, featuring four statues at the base and one atop a shaft, honors "Our Comrades" and was erected by U.S. Grant Post 28 of the Grand Army of the Republic (*left*). One of several Chicagoland monuments to a fraternal organization, this one at Elmwood Cemetery is dedicated to the Knights of Pythias (*below*).

ELMWOOD CEMETERY
2905 Thatcher Avenue
River Grove
773/625-1700

One of two largely Greek-American cemeteries in the Chicago area, this River Grove site is, on a fair night, something to behold. Hundreds of candles scattered throughout the cemetery set the darkness glimmering, reassuring passers-by of the brilliance of resurrection set against the blackness of death.

In addition to Greek sections and those nearby of Germans and Swedes, the cemetery also hosts gatherings of Albanians, Russians, Ukrainians, Bulgarians, Macedonians, Gypsies, and others, whose mourners have easily traveled to Elmwood via railroad from its earliest days.

Comedian **John Belushi** (1949-1982), still deeply mourned by his sweet home Chicago, has a cenotaph at this cemetery, although his remains lie elsewhere. The beloved Belushi, a veteran of influential local comedy company, The Second City, went on to help make a new television show, *Saturday Night Live*, the rage of a generation. But Belushi really distinguished himself as Chicago's own with the release of the Hollywood film, *The Blues Brothers,* in which he brought his singing, dancing, ex-convict character of Joliet Jake Blues to life on the streets of the city he loved. Though Chicago is today a filmmakers' town extraordinaire, *The Blues Brothers* was the first film to showcase the rich atmosphere and culture of the Windy City. In it, Chicagoans found a common ground and private jokes that have made the movie and its soundtrack—featuring a slew of rhythm and blues and soul masters, plus Belushi's wailing vocals—among Chicagoans' most sincerely valued pop-cultural treasures.

FOREST HOME/GERMAN WALDHEIM CEMETERY

863 South Desplaines Avenue
Forest Park
708/366-1900
Est. 1876

T his Forest Park gem, pierced by the Des Plaines River and spanning more than 200 acres, is the final home to nearly 190,000 dead, including local, national, and international notables from an array of arenas.

A mere *one-thirtieth* of the population of the Village of Forest Park is alive. The residents of its five cemeteries—Jewish Waldheim, Woodlawn, Concordia, Altenheim, and Forest Home/German Waldheim—make up the difference.

Hundreds of years after the ebbing of prehistoric Lake Chicago, the Potawatomi buried their dead in traditional mounds along the Des Plaines, one of which remains today as part of Forest Home. With the 1833 Treaty of Chicago and the end of the Black Hawk War came the relocation of the Potawatomi to lands west of the Mississippi. After this clearing of the land, the territory was open for bids during the public sale of northern Illinois land in the 1830s. Leon Bourassa, a French-Indian trapper, secured part of modern-day Forest Home; legend holds that his Potawatomi wife wanted to remain near her family's gravesite. Later, Ferdinand Haase, a Prussian immigrant, purchased a portion of the land and put down domestic and literal roots, building a home and raising crops as part of his living. When one of his only neighbors, brother-in-law Carl Zimmerman, died in 1854, he was buried on site, becoming the first white to be laid to rest in the soil of the future cemetery.

After transforming his postcard-perfect homestead into a successful public park, Haase thought he had it made. Problems with boisterous visitors, however, soon ruined his plan, forcing Haase to look for an alternative use for his land. Happily, his chagrin was perfectly coordinated with both the closing of the Chicago City Cemetery and the Chicago Common Council's ban on the development of new cemeteries inside the city limits.

Haase was poised to develop a new cemetery on his property. Earlier, he had arranged for the Galena & Chicago Union Railroad (later the Chicago and North Western) to run a spur from their tracks to his picnic grounds to facilitate the movement of pleasure-seekers to and from the park. Such a line would ensure funeral parties and visitors swift access to the cemetery from Chicago.

Haase piled all his confidence behind his speculation and began to sell his property to would-be cemetery developers. A first portion went to German Lutherans, who established Concordia Cemetery in 1872, and then another to an organization of German fraternal lodges, who founded German Waldheim one year later. Finally, a group of leading citizens of the Oak Park settlement proposed the development of a non-sectarian cemetery for the English-speaking upper classes of the region. The result was the cemetery called Forest Home (the English for "Waldheim"), established in 1876. Today, after more than a century of additions, Forest Home is an eclectic mix of burial customs and funerary art, testimony to the vast array of cultural groups represented by its population.

Here, as elsewhere, ethnic groups are sometimes gathered in their own sections. For example, just inside the cemetery gates are a number of elaborate monuments to the families of Gypsies who formerly held their local burials west of the Des Plaines River. Visitors will recognize the monuments by the photographs, gifts, food, and drink that typically adorn Gypsy graves. Further inside the cemetery, the **Cambrian Society** plot is a gathering spot for the deceased of Welsh ancestry.

Various veterans groups have found communal rest at Forest Home, their graves gathered around sometimes stunning central markers. The **Grand Army of the Republic, Phil Sheridan Post 615**, was formed in 1887 and erected its Forest Home monument in 1921. This memorial, the only one in the Chicago area to include an iron mortar affixed to its peak, stands sentinel over a number of its hundreds of members, inscribed with the

passage

ETERNAL VIGILANCE IS THE PRICE OF LIBERTY.

A substantial number of war veterans are gathered in a **Field of Honor**, complete with a memorial plaque, flagpole, and rows of flush stones. The Field was dedicated by the War Veterans Council of Oak Park in the early 1960s and was designed to improve on the tradition of placing flags on the individual graves of veterans on Memorial Day.

A number of labor unions and fraternal organizations have gathered their deceased members at Forest Home. Overseeing all of them is the **Haymarket Martyrs' Monument**, dedicated on June 25, 1893, and recently designated a National Historic Landmark by the U.S. Department of the Interior—the only cemetery marker in the country to receive such a distinction. The monument commemorates the four workers killed during Chicago's Haymarket Riot of May 1886, which was staged to protest police brutality. Ironically, in addition to the four worker casualties, seven policemen died.

The Haymarket Martyrs' Monument: The figure of Victory places a wreath on the head of a fallen worker. Four men were unjustly hanged on accusations of instigating the 1886 Haymarket Riot, an event that sparked labor movements worldwide.

Eight activists stood

trial in the aftermath, and all eight were declared guilty, though a number of those charged were not actually present at the Haymarket Square uprising. Five of the activists were sentenced to be hanged; only four were executed as one committed suicide while awaiting death. The remaining three activists were imprisoned.

Several years later, Governor John Peter Altgeld reviewed the case at the request of Clarence Darrow among others and granted pardons to the surviving prisoners, who were then released. When these, too, eventually died, they were buried with the executed at German Waldheim.

International anarchist and free speech advocate Emma Goldman, whose early life was influenced by the Haymarket incident, chose to be buried next to her heroes.

Also in this section, with her husband Albert (one of the executed Haymarket activists), is Texas native **Lucy Parsons** (1853-1942). In 1885, the Mexican-African-American reformer led a group of laborers down Prairie Avenue, demonstrating for the eight-hour workday and other improvements in labor conditions.

Near the Haymarket monument is the grave of Soviet revolutionary **Emma Goldman** (1869-1940), who requested burial here, close to her ideological siblings. Though she died in Canada after being barred from reentering the United States, Goldman's family was permitted to bury the anarchist here in Illinois.

A brick road passes in front of a row of mausoleums built into the side of a ridge of earth (*above*); another row is behind, facing the opposite direction. Several of these hillside mausoleums have had their doors removed or have been otherwise vandalized, including this one at the end of the ridge (*below*).

Looking quite eerie after a century of weathering, the Schmidt children, Lars and Ruth, continue to receive gifts of toys and flowers from visitors (*right*). A two-lane bridge provided a connection between the two halves of the cemetery separated by the Des Plaines River. The bridge is now closed for safety, blocked by a fence reading "May your crossing be blessed with eternal rest" (*below*).

The monument of the United Ancient Order of Druids features, of course, a druid, seated atop a tall pedestal. On the ground around him are three concentric circles of stone, carved to resemble wood (*right*). The largest tomb in Forest Home (*below*) is unoccupied and has no inscriptions other than 1902, its date of construction. Behind it, a stairway descends to an open door that permits access to the litter-strewn vault beneath.

A monument to the **International Alliance of Bill Posters and Billers, Local #1** commemorates a modest union of negligibly skilled laborers, who nonetheless organized in order to secure the privileges of union membership, including burial benefits. The memorial to the **Cigar Makers International Union, Local #14** features the grave of American Federation of Labor founder, **Adolph Strasser** (1844-1939). And the **Independent Order of Odd Fellows**, the first fraternal order in America to offer burial as part of its membership benefits, commissioned an impressive monument for its deceased brothers. Odder by far is that dedicated by the **United Ancient Order of Druids**, a centuries-old order based on the religious beliefs and practices of ancient Celtic tribes. In the 1880s, Chicago could boast more than a dozen local U.A.O.D. lodges or "Groves"; the order followed the lead of other, more traditional fraternal groups in providing a common burial site for its members.

Fans of American literary culture will find many diversions at Forest Home, including the graves of **Clarence** (1871-1928) **and Grace** (1872-1951) **Hemingway**, parents of Ernest. Also buried here is **Martha Louise Rayne** (1836-1911), the pioneering journalist who interviewed Mary Todd Lincoln during Mrs. Lincoln's stay in a Batavia, Illinois mental institution and who photographed the Beechers during Henry Ward's adultery trial.

Theater-lovers can visit the grave of famed impresario **Michael Todd** (1903-1958), onetime husband of Elizabeth Taylor, among other accomplishments; dance aficionados can seek out the grave of **Doris Humphrey** (1895-1958), modern dance pioneer.

Forest Home is also the everlasting home of premier evangelist, **Billy Sunday** (1862-1935). William Ashley Sunday, grandson of German immigrants, supported himself with odd jobs before being picked up by Chicago White Stockings manager, "Cap" Anson. Anson recruited the lightning-fast Sunday, who played with the Chicago team for eight years. During his athletic career, Sunday was born again, courtesy of Chicago's Pacific Garden Mission, whose hymns eventually inspired Billy to quit baseball to assist an evangelist. After five years of such work,

Adolph J. Sabath (*above*), a Jewish immigrant from Bohemia, served 23 consecutive terms in the U.S. Congress. (*Below*) This classical mausoleum houses the Grunow family, founders of the Majestic Radio Corporation. On the sides are statues of Hermes and Athena, as the Spirit of Commerce and the Spirit of Radio. The Des Plaines River is only a few feet behind.

Sunday became a minister himself, taking his signature no-holds-barred style on the road to revival meetings, where he condemned drinking, smoking, birth control, and other contemporary "scourges." Frank Sinatra later sang of Chicago as the town Sunday "couldn't put down." In fact, it was Chicago that at last put Sunday down—six feet down, to be exact—when he died of a heart attack in 1935.

Western suburbanites will recognize far more folks here than the nationally and internationally renowned personalities mentioned above. Along with **Ferdinand Haase** (1826-1911), first owner of this very parcel of land, a number of prominent and popular local personalities are buried at this now-populous site.

James Fletcher Skinner (1868-1917), **Edwin Gale** (1832-1913), **Sophy Sievert** (1875-1953) **and Charles** (1873-1925) **Dreschler, Flora Gill** (1848-1934), and **Adolph Westphal** (1835-1913): these local entrepreneurs, all reposing together at Forest Home, were largely responsible for nurturing the commerce of the western suburbs during the towns' formative days. A number of their graves are marked by some of the most impressive monuments in the area. Most notable is that of **Edmund Cummings** (1842-1922), who made his name in founding the Cicero & Proviso Street Railway Company, an electric streetcar line, and watched his initial effort bloom into the West Town Bus Company, which served many of the suburbs and subdivisions that his real estate development firm had initiated. The Cummings family monument, at one time the most lavish in the cemetery, was designed by Louis Comfort Tiffany during the rage for Egyptian stylization in 1922, the year of the rediscovery of King Tut's tomb. Though Tiffany's glass pieces embellish many Chicago mausoleums, the Cummings memorial is the only known existing Tiffany monument in the metropolitan area.

One of the many gates into the Jewish Waldheim cemetery complex (*above*).
Most of the congregations and other organizations with their own sections would
erect special gates of brick, stone, or iron. As in many other Jewish cemeteries, the
monuments are very close together, and many have porcelain photographs affixed to
them (*below*). In the older sections, west of Des Plaines Avenue, the paths are long
and narrow, and the more remote sections can be reached only after a long walk.

JEWISH WALDHEIM CEMETERY
1800 South Harlem Avenue
Forest Park
708/366-4541
Jewish

When Chicago's Jewish population began its westward movement, some may have anticipated that the western suburbs would ultimately become a prime destination for Jewish migrants from Chicago. Yet, though the concentration of Jews in the old Maxwell Street ghetto rapidly thinned, transplanted to neighborhoods like Lawndale, Austin, Douglas, and Garfield Park, points further west never became a popular target. One reason was the already huge populations of a number of these western suburbs. Due to their proximity to the city center, many of these villages, such as Maywood and Oak Park, had already hosted significant prewar settlement, leaving little room for new mass migrations. Additionally, places like Berwyn and Cicero were overwhelmingly blue-collar towns.

Even now, a mere 15,000 Jews live in the western suburbs, yet the largest of the 13 Jewish cemeteries in the Chicago area is here in Forest Park, part of the sprawling burial ground known vaguely as Waldheim. Jewish Waldheim was founded during the second wave of Jewish immigration to Chicago in the mid- to late-19th century. While the first group of settlers had been Germanic, quickly conforming to American ways, the second migration was comprised of Eastern European Jews, who were typically more conservative and less eager to be assimilated into American culture. Insisting on their own cemeteries, congregations eagerly purchased the plots offered by their synagogues, opting for burial in places like Waldheim, which was never a single cemetery but rather a gathering of the communal plots of more than 300 congregations, *vereins*, and *landsmanschaften*, at one time rigidly divided by gated fences, some of which remain. Initially intriguing for this sectionalization, the thousands of

A small mausoleum, inscribed with Hebrew lettering (*above*).
Built-up mounds of earth cover many graves and are
often planted with flowers in season (*below*).

The gate of the Warsaw Benevolent Association Cemetery (*above*). As Jewish law requires burial in earth, mausoleums are uncommon at Jewish Waldheim. One of the largest of the cemetery's mausoleums is that of Ida Balaban Katz, of the Balaban-Katz theater chain (*below*).

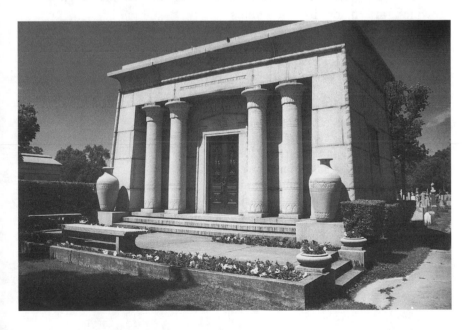

monuments spanning many ethnicities, and the *Bet-Taharas* once used for the preparation of bodies in the days before burial vaults, the cemetery is ultimately valued as a treasure cache of Chicago's Jewish history.

Waldheim's first Jewish interment was held in 1875; at that time, funeral parties and visitors faced a day-long excursion from the Maxwell Street neighborhood to the graves of their loved ones. In 1914, however, the Metropolitan Elevated began running a funeral route to Waldheim that operated successfully for two decades.

One of the most famous graves among the nearly 175,000 at this site is that of 18-year-old marine **Samuel Meisenberg** (d. 1914), the first American to be killed during the American military landings at Vera Cruz, Mexico. Meisenberg received the Purple Heart for his actions 75 years after his death.

Infinitely less deserved is the fame of another Jewish Waldheim plot: the grave of **Albert Weinshank** (1893-1929), who had been the newest member of Bugs Moran's gang when he was shot to death with six others in the St. Valentine's Day Massacre.

Upon leaving Jewish Waldheim, note the cemetery gates, which are made from columns taken from the old County Building, demolished in 1908.

The obelisk of Samuel "Nails" Morton, a member of the O'Banion/ Weiss gang in the early 1920s. Morton's success as a criminal was overshadowed by the story of his death: while riding in Lincoln Park, he was thrown from the horse, broke his neck, and died. Hymie Weiss, one of the most violent of Chicago gangsters, shot the horse, then phoned its owner and told him to come and pick up his saddle.

WOODLAWN CEMETERY
7600 Cermak Road
Forest Park
708/442-8500

This Forest Park burial ground is a hit with children; just ask them about the elephants in the cemetery.

Showmen's Rest, Woodlawn's biggest drawing card, is maintained by the Showmen's League of America for the burial of circus performers. Included among its resurrection-bound residents are 50 performers and crew members killed in a wreck of the Hagenbeck-Wallace Circus train near Hammond, Indiana in June 1918. Most of the headstones are marked with only nicknames, like "The Fat Man" or "Baldy," or with "Unknown" designations. Drawing the curious to this spot are five spectacularly somber stone elephants, their trunks lowered as if in mour-

Headstones for "4 Horse Driver" and "Baldy," victims in the 1918 Hagenbeck-Wallace Circus train wreck.

One of five stone
elephants that
are part of
"Showmen's Rest,"
a part of Woodlawn
maintained by the
Showmen's League
of America for the
burial of circus
performers.

ning—testimony to an unfounded legend that tells of the animals
rescuing victims from the deadly fire that consumed most of the
train wreck's victims.

Also buried here is **Ervin Dusak** (1920-1994), who played
for the Pittsburgh Pirates in the 1950s.

CONCORDIA CEMETERY

7900 Madison Street
Forest Park
708/366-0017
Protestant

This German Protestant Cemetery, also part of the Forest
Park community of burial grounds, was established after the
fashion of the German Roman Catholic sites. Protestants of Germanic ancestry desired their own cemeteries, separate from
those established sites that catered exclusively to their religion
but accepted deceased members of many ethnicities.

The impeccable surroundings at Concordia are made even
more elegant by the rare **carillon** on the grounds and a beautiful
limestone grapevine and marker commemorating a pair of
victims of the 1915 *Eastland* disaster.

Among the more popular monument types at Concordia are obelisks and small granite cylindrical headstones (*above*). Often, a group of these cylindrical headstones will be mounted on a common base stretching across the entire family plot. This unusual mausoleum (*below*) is tall enough to walk into at the front, but the roof curves downward at the rear until it is barely tall enough to accommodate a coffin.

ALTENHEIM CEMETERY
7824 Madison Street
Forest Park
Protestant

This burial ground adjacent to Concordia is the property of the German Old People's Home. Founded by a utopian society, very little variety may be found here in the way of grave decoration; the simple concrete markers seem rather to strive together for uniformity.

MOUNT AUBURN CEMETERY
4101 Oak Park Avenue
Stickney
773/242-1466

Although an Oriental shrine stands sentinel over one of the newer sections, Mt. Auburn Cemetery in Stickney, home to a substantial population of Chinese-Americans, is missing the traditional signs of Chinese burial. Typical Chinese-American monuments are slim and vertical, often stamped with photographs and inscribed with Chinese characters. Here at Mt. Auburn, however, cemetery regulations, demanding the use of simple flush stones, have proscribed the more customary memorials. The shrine, used for seasonal ceremonial offerings, remains the sole indicator of the site's ethnic bent.

Another notable monument here is called "The Living Lord." The face of Christ is sculpted as a negative—that is, features that would ordinarily be closest to the viewer are instead furthest away. The resulting effect is that the face seems to always be looking toward the audience when viewed from any direction, an optical illusion unique among Chicago cemeteries.

MOUNT EMBLEM CEMETERY
510 West Grand Avenue
Elmhurst
630/834-6080

Wedding parties as well as funeral corteges gather at this Elmhurst site for portraits in front of the authentic circa 1865 windmill that is the unmistakable emblem of Mt. Emblem.

Originally a Masonic cemetery, this site now hosts a variety of burials, drawn by the cemetery's unusually placid surroundings.

ELM LAWN CEMETERY
401 East Lake Street
Elmhurst
630/833-9696

Animal lovers will appreciate a peculiar burial custom at this Elmhurst cemetery: the interment of pets with their owners. For the slightly less eccentric, separate pet burial is available here as well.

Another unusual feature is the cemetery's **Zoroastrian section**, where most of the markers display the likeness of the creator, Ahuru-Mazda.

ARLINGTON CEMETERY
Lake Street & Frontage Road
Elmhurst
630/832-2599

This serene Elmhurst site provides fitting repose for the Modern Woodmen of America, whose memorial keeps company with monuments to Bartenders and Waiters, among others. The Modern Woodmen were founded in the 1880s by Iowan Joseph Cullen Root, whose vision of a self-governing society fed by nationwide "camps" was realized in the formation of a fraternal benefit society. Not associated with forestry, logging, or other such professions, the group's misleading name was inspired by a sermon heard by Root, in which his minister evoked a spiritual analogy involving pioneer woodmen clearing away a forest. Aiming to help members clear their financial responsibilities before death, Root seized upon the image and christened his society Modern Woodmen, later adding "of America" to include the patriotic bent of the group's membership.

The public became acquainted with the Woodmen during the 1904 World's Fair at St. Louis, when the Modern Woodmen Foresters, an axe-wielding drill team, dazzled audiences with their colorful garb and clever performances. The team's popularity continued to grow, with local appearances in parades and competitions across the country leading to a presidential audience with Herbert Hoover. Unfortunately, World War I resulted in the dissolution of the Foresters. They would never reassemble again.

Despite their retreat from the public spotlight, the Woodmen continued to shine. From 1909 to 1947, the fraternity operated a tuberculosis sanitarium in the Rocky Mountain foothills outside of Colorado Springs with tremendous success. More than 12,000 members were treated during those years, more than 70 percent of whom recovered. The treatment? The era's recommended medicine of clean air and exercise.

OAK RIDGE CEMETERY
4301 West Roosevelt Road
Hillside
708/344-5600

Harold **Lincoln Gray** (1894-1968), local suburban boy and creator of Li'l Orphan Annie, established his hollow-eyed heroine on the pages of the *Chicago Tribune.* He is buried at this Hillside site.

And **Howlin' Wolf** (1910-1976), born Chester A. Burnett, was laid to rest here in 1976, after nearly 70 years of exceptionally hard living. Hailing from Mississippi, Howlin' Wolf's earliest form of musical expression involved singing in church on Sunday. At the age of 18, however, he was given a guitar by his father. Almost simultaneously, Chester met a man named Charley Patton, a Delta Blues pioneer who took Chester under his wing and taught the youngster according to his own unique style. For several years, Chester honed his skills for patrons of the local weekly fish fries, spending his days farming with his family. After moving to Arkansas, Chester met another Delta Blues performer, Sonny Boy Williamson, who taught him the

harmonica. Not long after, Chester quit farming and took his show on the road. After several years of wayfaring and another four in the service, he returned to farming, only to abandon it once again to form his own band and return to the road. Though Chester gained a solid following in Mississippi and Arkansas, it wasn't until he was 38 years old that he landed the radio spot in West Memphis which made him a sensation and led to a recording contract with Chicago's Chess Records in 1950 for his cut, "How Many More Years" and "Moanin' at Midnight." After the record sold a whopping 60,000 copies, RPM began competing with Chess for Wolf's recordings. Chess won. And Chess, Chester, and the Chicago Blues became thoroughly entwined.

At 6 feet 6 inches and nearly 300 pounds, with an earth-shaking voice punctuated by gut-wrenching moans and wails, Chester Burnett had become a performer known for scaring audiences out of their wits. In the years since his debut, he has been credited by hundreds of musicians, representing countless countries and musical styles, as a major influence on their work.

Chester continued his popular performances throughout his later years of kidney trouble, receiving dialysis before beginning his engagements. He died in Chicago, the town that loved him well, on January 10, 1976.

For fraternal historians, and brothers, the Mason's Rest monument at Oak Ridge is a lovely place to stop.

MOUNT CARMEL CEMETERY

1400 South Wolf Road
Hillside
708/449-8300
Catholic, Est. 1901

Located in the near western suburb of Hillside, this lavishly decorated, predominantly Italian cemetery contains perhaps the most eclectic slate of personalities to be found in the Chicago metropolitan area.

Not many Chicagoans had ever seen the inside of the **Bishops Mausoleum** at Mt. Carmel until the death of **Joseph Cardinal Bernardin** (1928-1996) in the fall of 1996. The mosaic-encrusted interior of the hilltop structure became home to the body of Chicago's Archbishop after his much-publicized battle with pancreatic cancer. Throughout his illness, Bernardin won the acclaim of countless observers from all walks of life, writing and speaking on his struggle to accept his imminent death and emphasizing the need for reconciliation and faith in attaining the peace and joy he had found on the threshold of that death.

After his passing, Bernardin lay in state for three days in Holy Name Cathedral, as 100,000 mourners lined up around the block to pay their last respects to this remarkable leader.

The Bishops' Mausoleum at the center of Mount Carmel. Above the door is written "Resurrecturis."

Though guards at this wake began their watch in trying to keep mournful hands from touching the casket and body, they soon abandoned their duty after the throngs persisted in their efforts; the result was a symbolically soiled casket, well suited to the funeral procession, which would travel, not swiftly over the expressways, but laboriously through the streets of Chicago, as the Cardinal had insisted.

After much dignified but down-to-earth fanfare, Bernardin was interred with other Church dignitaries, including **Bishop Quarter** (1806-1848), **Archbishops Feehan** (1829-1902) **and Quigley** (1854-1915), and predecessor **Joseph Cardinal Cody** (1907-1982), in Mt. Carmel's Bishop's Mausoleum, drawing thousands to the site during the winter of 1996-97, when the cemetery extended the hours for public viewing due to the Bernardin burial. The interior of the Mausoleum is still open on Sundays several months of the year; the exterior is always accessible during regular cemetery visitation hours.

Also popular at Mt. Carmel is the grave of a young mother named **Julia Buccola Petta** (d. 1921, age 29), locally known as "The Italian Bride." After dying in childbirth, Buccola was buried with her baby. Dreams of Julia haunted her mother, however, who often envisioned her daughter begging to be disinterred. After seven years, the woman finally gave in to her nightmares and had Julia's coffin unearthed. Upon its opening, all were shocked to discover that, although the baby was completely decomposed, Julia remained perfectly intact. To commemorate the supposed miracle, the family had  two porcelain portraits added to Julia's marker: one of the girl in life, the other of Julia lying in her casket, seven years after her death.

Mt. Carmel serves not only as the slumber-ground of saints but as a last hideout of some of the most notorious characters in gangland history, among them, **Alphonse "Al" Capone** (1899-1947).

Capone was born in Brooklyn, the fourth of nine children of Italian immigrants. He abandoned his education in sixth grade, when he received a beating from the school principal for thrashing his own tutor. He joined up with the James Street Gang, a bunch of adolescent thugs headed by John Torrio, who would later become the first of the Chicago bootleggers. Torrio put Al to work as a bouncer for a brothel and bar in their home borough. Here, he tangled with a punk named Frank Galluccio, who slashed Capone's left cheek, gaining him the immortal identification of "Scarface."

Capone fled arrest to Chicago to reunite with Torrio, who was up in arms about his uncle, gangster head "Big" Jim Colosimo, who was reluctant to involve himself in the business of bootlegging. Capone and Torrio had Big Jim killed by a team of New York hit men.

Torrio and Capone took over the Chicago outfit, presenting a solid front of murder to any local gang that wouldn't recognize their ultimate authority. It was Dion O'Banion's gang, in particular, that put up the toughest fight against the partnership and at

last landed Torrio himself in the hospital. Torrio recovered and moved back to New York, leaving his boyhood friend with full command of the Chicago Mob.

Capone was 26 years old.

After making a fortune through bootlegging, prostitution, and gambling rackets and orchestrating countless murders of uncooperative or disloyal colleagues and rivals, Capone was finally sent to prison—for tax evasion. He split his sentence between the federal penitentiary in Atlanta and Alcatraz Island, where he suffered a number of attempts on his life, including efforts of his co-convicts to strangle, poison, and stab him to death. But it was Al's own life that finally killed him; an early bout with syphilis spread to his brain and rendered him utterly helpless during his final days. He died in the same Florida home where he had been when his men carried out the St. Valentine's Day Massacre of 1929.

Capone's simple grave marker has been stolen at least twice—at 125 pounds, a risky and weighty souvenir. But don't blame any of the other underworld denizens also buried here, who are, these days, as inactive as old Al.

The **Genna Family** tree produced an abundant harvest of ne'er-do-wells, including Pete, Sam, Vincenzo ("Jim"), and of course, "Bloody" Angelo, Tony "The Gentleman," and Mike "The Devil," who made the rounds of gangster circles before ending up here at Mt. Carmel.

Also here to stay is choir boy and florist **Dion "Deanie" O'Banion** (1892-1924), who moved swiftly from the Little Hell district (bounded by Chicago Avenue, Wells Street, Division Street, and the Chicago River) of north side Chicago into infamy. As a kid, O'Banion spent his nights in brothels and bars, eventually landing jobs as a singing waiter in the near north hovels along Erie and Clark streets, moaning weepy Irish folk songs and picking the pockets of his drunken listeners. Supplementing his income by mugging pedestrians after closing time, O'Banion was arrested in 1909, spending several months in prison. A couple of years later, he was arrested for the second and last time for concealment of a weapon. After this final stint, Dion stuck to the Chicago system of avoiding arrest for his crimes, regularly

paying off the local authorities to ensure his future freedom.

O'Banion's reformed life brought him a job manhandling newspaper vendors for the *Chicago Tribune*, encouraging hawkers to push the local daily, for their own good. While working the same racket for the Hearst newspaper group, Charlie Reiser took the fragile youngster under his wing, teaching him the art of safecracking.

But it was Prohibition that really nurtured Dion's dormant talents. Emerging as the head honcho of the so-called North Siders, O'Banion led a motley crew, including such low-life luminaries as "Bugs" Moran. Together they hijacked shipments of alcohol produced by bootlegger John Torrio, re-routing them to the burgeoning speakeasies. When demand outgrew their supply, the North Siders seized a number of local breweries, but continued to steal Torrio's turnout. The bootlegger grew increasingly incensed.

Suddenly, O'Banion offered to sell Torrio the local Sieben Brewery for a half million clams and to leave him to do business in peace. Stunned, Torrio practically threw the money at Dion, after which the Feds stormed the brewery and charged the bewildered businessman with violation of Prohibition laws. When he discovered that O'Banion had known about the Feds' plan to seize the business, and had turned it into a moneymaking scheme to his own benefit, Torrio began to think of revenge.

That revenge came one fall morning while O'Banion was busy at his flower shop on north State Street, a legitimate front from which he filled orders for gangland funerals. Three men arrived to pick up an arrangement for the funeral of mobster Mike Merlo and, while O'Banion was graciously shaking hands with one of them, the remaining two shot him six times. It was

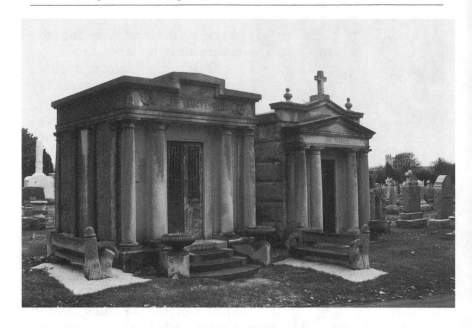

Mount Carmel has over 400 family mausoleums such as these (*above*), a visible indicator of the cemetery's Italian heritage. The mausoleum of Mob boss Sam Giancana (*below*), who was killed in his own house.

Francesco Salerno, age 7. His monument (*left*) was created by faithfully reproducing the photograph that appears on the front, left. Even the details of the chair and the folds of his clothing were duplicated exactly. (*Below*) Mount Carmel's most unusual monument is that of the Di Salvo family, reproduced here as an extraordinarily detailed marble sculpture. The top of this monument rotates 360 degrees on the base.

payback time for Torrio and the end of O'Banion's reign.

A key colleague of O'Banion was a Polish immigrant named Earl Wajciechowski. After their arrival in Chicago, the family changed their name to Weiss and began to make a life in their new city. Son Earl soon met up with the teenaged Dion, and together hooligan O'Banion and **"Hymie" Weiss** (1898-1926) pulled off numerous car thefts and burglaries before moving on to more "legitimate" paid jobs muscling newspaper vendors.

As O'Banion's closest associate, Weiss took over leadership of the North Siders after his boss's murder by Torrio's henchmen. At barely 28 years old, his primary order of business was to avenge O'Banion by rubbing out those he felt were responsible: John Torrio and Al Capone. After two unsuccessful attempts on Torrio's life and numerous failures to rub out Capone, Weiss was killed by a sniper who opened fire from the window over O'Banion's old flower shop. Weiss is buried at Mt. Carmel with his boyhood chum.

Joining O'Banion and Weiss in the cemetery is a rival mobster: the fastest gun in Chicago history, **"Machine Gun Jack" McGurn**.

Born and raised **James Vincenzo DeMora** (1904-1936), the young Chicago native was an upstanding family man until the Genna gang killed his father **Angelo DeMora** (d. 1923) for selling bootleg alcohol behind their backs. According to a local legend, James drenched his hands in the blood of his father and became obsessed with avenging his murder. After self-instruction in marksmanship and training as a boxer, the contender known as "Battling Jack McGurn" joined Capone's gang.

McGurn's expertise in handling the so-called tommy gun earned him a high place among Capone's cronies. Al chose him often for his biggest hit jobs and, in time, Jack would number among his 25 commissioned homicides six members of the Genna gang. When he did away with the Gennas, McGurn placed in each of their stiffening hands a five-cent piece, identifying them as "lousy nickel and dimers."

Yet though the death of the Gennas satisfied his deep personal vendetta, it was his role in the St. Valentine's Day Massacre that made McGurn a legend. Rumored to have been the lead gunman and orchestrator of the massacre, McGurn was arrested in connection with the operation, but cleared by the testimony of girlfriend Louise Rolfe who furnished an alibi. When Rolfe's story was disproved, McGurn was charged with perjury, then prevented Rolfe from testifying against him by marrying her before the trial.

Left on his own after Capone went off to prison, McGurn unwisely turned to narcotics trafficking and was gunned down in a bowling alley by two strangers on the night before Valentine's Day. Authorities found a nickel pressed into his palm and, beside his body, a grotesque valentine reading

> *You've lost your job,*
> *You've lost your dough,*
> *Your jewels and handsome houses.*
> *But things could be worse, you know,*
> *At least you have your trousers.*

The conflicting clues embedded in the jingle left police baffled. Was the culprit seeking remorse for the Genna deaths, as suggested by the palmed nickel? Or was the grisly valentine a token from someone determined to pay back McGurn for his role in the February 14th massacre? The puzzle remains unsolved.

Despite his rise and fall in the pages of gangland history, James DeMora did achieve some legitimate success, which continues to this day. While "Machine Gun Jack" McGurn became a legend owing to his strong-armed exploits, he has been beloved by local nightclubbers for decades. DeMora's "real" job involved ownership of a string of cabarets, among them the still-stompin' Uptown fixture, The Green Mill.

Rounding out the roster at Mt. Carmel are gangland loveables **John May** (d. 1929), **Frank "The Enforcer" Nitti** (1884-1943), **Roger Touhy** (1898-1959), Capone advisor **Antonio "The Scourge" Lombardo** (1892-1928), and **Sam "Mooney" Giancana** (1908-1975), ruthless successor to Tony Accardo, boss of Chicago's Mafia.

Still not enough to sate your quest for infamy? No problem; simply cross the street to Queen of Heaven Cemetery.

QUEEN OF HEAVEN CEMETERY
1400 South Wolf Road
Hillside
708/449-8300
Catholic, Est. 1947

Here you'll find the plots of such sterling citizens as Mob boss, **Sam Battaglia** (1908-1973), a teddy bear compared to his predecessor, Giancana.

Queen of Heaven is also the dead end for another Capone cohort, **Paul "The Waiter" Ricca** (1897-1972). Ricca began his mob life in high style by murdering his sister's ex-boyfriend, Emilio Perillo, when Perillo's family openly disapproved of the Ricca clan. Imprisoned for the deed, Ricca emerged from stir two years later and immediately demonstrated his remorse by killing Vencenzo Capasso, the eyewitness that had put Ricca behind bars.

After emigrating from Naples to the United States via a careful route of escape through France, Ricca traveled to Chicago and began working as a waiter for "Diamond" Joe Esposito. A Mob hangout, Esposito's restaurant was a fine place to be for a young go-getter like Paul. He soon became friends with a select group of patrons and left Esposito's to run the World Playhouse, a venue owned by Al Capone. The Mob boss and his new charge became fast and lasting friends, so much so that, when Ricca was married in 1927, Capone served as his best man.

Though Ricca was involved in many of the Mob's Chicago plans, he spent much of his time on the East Coast, serving as something of an ambassador for Al Capone. He made the national spotlight in the 1940s, however, for his involvement in the so-called "Hollywood Extortion Case," in which Ricca and others had been found blackmailing the motion picture studios by threatening the striking of the Mob-controlled Projectionists Union if the studios didn't pay off big. When two of the extortionists were charged, they squealed on the others. Paul Ricca and others were indicted. But when Frank Nitti, then head of the Chicago Mob, killed himself over the consequences, Ricca found himself the new leader of the local Outfit.

Ricca's reign was a short one. Found guilty of extortion, he was sent to Leavenworth for ten years. Next in line for the Chicago throne was Tony Accardo.

After serving only three years and four months, during which time he communicated constantly with Accardo, Ricca was paroled. Because he could not associate with known gangsters due to parole restrictions, Ricca was officially "out" of the Mob. Though his exploits went undercover, he was finally nabbed for his first crime when Immigration and Naturalization Services exposed Ricca as Italian fugitive, Felice DeLucia. Ricca was issued a deportation order after having his citizenship revoked, but he struggled to remain in the United States. After many tactics, both shady and solid, he succeeded in having the order dropped.

"The Waiter" passed away in the early 1970s from natural causes and joined his cohorts in a plot at Queen of Heaven.

But neither Battaglia or Ricca can hold a candle to the legacy of one **Antonio Accardo** (1906-1992), the original "Big Tuna," otherwise known as "Joe Batters."

Antonio Leonardo Accardo grew up in Chicago's Little Sicily, his parents having immigrated around the turn of the century. When Antonio failed to show progress in the classroom, Mom and Dad filed a delayed birth record affidavit, placing his birth in 1904 rather than 1906 and rendering him fit to legally drop out of school. Not two years later, Accardo was arrested for a motor vehicle violation; his life of crime had begun.

The next year, Tony was fined for disorderly conduct at a pool hall and joined the Circus Cafe Gang, where he mixed with such members as Claude Maddox and James DeMora. Like many would-be gangland greats, Accardo started out pickpocketing and jumping passers-by, moving on to armed robbery, jewel and car theft, and other specialties. Then real opportunities came with the advent of Prohibition, when the delivery boy began using his truck to deliver booze from Sicilian family stills to Chicago's speakeasies. Finally, Accardo got his big break when boyhood buddy DeMora—who had since been picked up as a hit man for Al Capone—put in a good word for Tony at the office.

Capone called Accardo to his office at the Metropole Hotel, leading him in swearing the oath which would make him an official member of the Chicago Mob.

Capone's eyes shone at the loyalty of the new recruit. During Hymie Weiss's siege of Capone's Hawthorn Inn in Cicero, Accardo pulled his boss to the ground, lying on top of him to protect him from the thousands of rounds of machine gun fire that were showering the building. After this impressive display of devotion, Accardo could often be seen in the lobby of the Hawthorn, armed and awaiting any further attempts on the life of his leader.

Accardo continued to win the esteem of his boss in equally unorthodox ways. In fact, the plucky underling earned his most famous nickname when sponsor Jack McGurn reported to Capone that Tony had ruthlessly smashed the skulls of two adversaries with a baseball bat, prompting the boss to comment that Accardo was "a real Joe Batters."

Accardo made bona fide history when he was ordered to storm the SMC Cartage Company garage on north Clark Street on Valentine's Day of 1929 and with the help of three associates do away with "Bugs" Moran and a key portion of his gang. Disguised as police officers, Al's four delegates entered the garage, spraying the seven men there with machine gun fire. Though Moran himself had been running late to the rendezvous and thus eluded his fate, six of his men died immediately; the seventh miraculously survived long enough to reach the hospital, where he died without squealing on his assailants.

The Big Tuna continued to distinguish himself as a mobster's mobster, remaining faithful to his boss, Capone, throughout the leader's prison term, carrying out assignments and stepping in as gangland leader when circumstances called for his authority.

When Accardo at last tired of Mob rule, he petitioned for an out and got it. Handing the family reigns to Sam Giancana, Joe Batters retired into the consulting business, as it were, living out his last years overseeing the Chicago Mob. Upon his death, Accardo was buried at Mt. Carmel, in proper Italian style.

But don't be fooled by the few bad seeds at this handsomely

Several victims of the fire at Our Lady of the Angels school are buried near this monument.

landscaped headquarters of Chicago's Archdiocesan Cemeteries. The innocent easily outnumber the guilty.

In fact, this is the site of **The Shrine of the Holy Innocents**, a section reserved for the burials of children. Many visitors travel to the shrine to offer their prayers at the **Our Lady of the Angels Memorial** dedicated to the victims of one of the worst tragedies in Chicago's history, the 1958 school fire which took the lives of 92 children and three nuns. The bodies of 25 of these children rest at this special site, a triangular portion of land marked by a striking monument bearing the names of all the fire's victims.

Queen of Heaven is also host to the more than 20,000 souls interred in its **Community Mausoleum**. One of the largest in the United States, the enormous crypt is also a stunning gallery, filled with panes of beautiful stained glass.

Though mourners are plentiful at this sacred and spacious burial site, the most frequent visitors come not to spend a quiet moment at a loved one's plot, but to take part in a curious phenomenon that has centered on the cemetery for nearly a decade: the Marian apparitions reported by retired railroad employee, Joseph Reinholtz.

In 1987, the widowed Reinholtz made a pilgrimage to the town of Medjugorje, Bosnia-Herzogovina, to pray at the site

Strong and Silent
The Catholic Cemeteries of Chicago

With 42 sites currently under its jurisdiction, the Catholic cemeteries of the Archdiocese of Chicago continue to provide a solid and ever-increasing local front against the onslaught of the corporate cemetery.

At last count, Archdiocesan cemeteries held 2.5 million graves and 128,000 crypts and niches, spread among more than 3,000 acres and 27 community mausoleums. From single-acre churchyards to sprawling ossuaries burying over 1,000 faithful a year, local Catholics have a dizzying array of funeral destinations to choose from. And they just keep coming.

The Archdiocese had a head start on the burial business; the oldest cemetery in the metropolitan area is the Catholic churchyard of St. James-Sag Bridge, in use from the early 1830s and still in operation, along with every one of the Catholic cemeteries opened since except the first Diocesan burial ground at North Avenue and Dearborn Street, whose burials were re-interred at Calvary Cemetery in Evanston upon the closing of the earliest city cemeteries during the 1860s.

The tremendous popularity of the Catholic cemeteries of Chicago increased dramatically after the consolidation of their control under Francis Cardinal Meyer during the 1960s. With a central authority dictating burial policy, pricing, maintenance, and regulations, the sites presented an appealingly reliable destination for those contemplating their own inevitable demise. The manicured elegance and glossy brochures of the new cemetery system seemed to promise comfort and care for those worried about the future of many local, independent sites that seemed to be falling under mismanagement or, worse yet, going wild.

During the Cardinal Bernardin years, a full 90 percent of the Archdiocesan Catholic population utilized at least one of the system's cemeteries. Some credit the huge majority to the system's recent emphasis on ethnic identification of individual cemeteries or separate sections within them catering to specific cultural groups. Dutifully tracking the ethnicity of their burials, the Archdiocesan cemeteries have been quick to cater to cultural sensibilities, erecting monuments to specific heritages and creating instant ethnic mini-settlements.

where six young people had been claiming visions of the Blessed Virgin. During his time in Medjugorje, one of the seers prayed over Reinholtz and, upon his return to the Chicago area, Joseph's failing sight returned suddenly when he beheld in his home a small statue of Mary weeping tears.

Returning to Bosnia in 1989, the visionary that had prayed over Reinholtz gave the American pilgrim a mission: Joseph was to return home and search for a crucifix next to a three-branched tree. There, he should pray.

Back in Hillside, Illinois, Reinholtz found the

Apparitions of the Virgin Mary have been reported near this cross, which continues to receive a steady stream of visitors.

spot in nearby Queen of Heaven Cemetery. He immediately began a determined vigil. Approximately one year after beginning his prayer at the "Trinity Tree," Joseph experienced his first apparition of the Blessed Virgin. Several months later, she returned to the site accompanied by the archangel, St. Michael.

Blissful, Joseph enthusiastically spread the news of his visions, and soon large numbers of pilgrims were joining him in his daily prayers at the site. Almost immediately, reports of strange phenomena began to issue from these gatherings. Visitors reported photographs containing vivid images of Mary and of angels, the strong scent of roses at the wintry cemetery site, secret conversations with heavenly beings, and other marvels. As evidence of the visions, they displayed their once battered and multicolored rosaries that had turned a glittering gold after visiting Queen of Heaven.

Soon, the Archdiocese of Chicago was called on to issue a statement regarding the apparitions. Though officials refrained from declaring the reality of the apparitions, the local Church continued to allow Reinholtz to visit the site, though placing on him a restriction of obedience forbidding visitation on Tuesdays. Joseph continued his almost daily visits to the crucifix and continued to receive monthly messages from the Blessed Virgin until he suffered a stroke in 1995.

For lighter relief, along with the cemetery's would-be saints and dreadful sinners are Chicago Bear **William Wightkin** (1927-1997) and comedian **George Kirby** (1925-1995), who settled in here after his last laugh.

Visitors should note the adjacent **Our Lady of Sorrows Cemetery** on this property, which is now under the care of the larger Queen of Heaven complex.

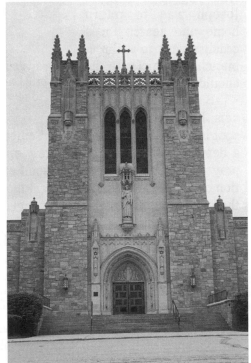

The central tower of the community mausoleum at Queen of Heaven is in the Gothic style.

HINSDALE ANIMAL CEMETERY
6400 Bentley Avenue
Clarendon Hills
630/323-5120

This intriguing Clarendon Hills expanse provides rest for more than dogs and cats. Grieving owners can pay their respects at Hinsdale Animal Cemetery to cherished birds, prize horses, loved monkeys, and other gone-but-not-forgotten pets from across the metropolitan area.

III. SOUTH

This angel is part of an elaborate Celtic Cross found
above a grave at Oak Woods Cemetery.

CITY SOUTH

The largest "white bronze" or zinc monument in the Chicago area
is at Oak Woods Cemetery and commemorates Paul Cornell, founder
of the town, now neighborhood, of Hyde park.

"Remember me as one who tried to be fair" reads the mausoleum of Harold Washington, first African-American mayor of Chicago (*above*). Also at Oak Woods, the notorious: "Big" Jim Colosimo was Chicago's top Mob boss until 1920 when he refused to take part in bootlegging. He was shot by an unknown killer thought to have been working for Colosimo's nephew, Johnny Torrio, and his associate, Al Capone (*below*).

OAK WOODS CEMETERY
1035 East 67th Street
Chicago
773/288-3800
Est. 1853

One of the city's oldest cemeteries, Oak Woods is part of Chicago's Woodlawn neighborhood. Situated at 67th Street and Cottage Grove Avenue, the burial ground was founded in 1853 and held its first burial in 1865. One year later, the Illinois Central began operation of a spur line to aid visitors, and new arrivals, in their travels to the cemetery. The Oak Woods Cemetery Association, intent on establishing the site as a progressive paradise, called in Adoph Strauch of Cincinnati's renowned Spring Grove Cemetery to oversee the development of the property. The trend toward park-like cemeteries assured that the site would be both expansive and naturalistic, but Strauch went a bit further at Oak Woods, trumpeting the so-called "lawn plan," which disallowed walls, curbs, or fences of any kind around lot edges. The result is a gorgeous example of 19th-century cemetery planning: a sloping park of hills and trees accented by a number of placid lakes and maneuverable via a system of gently snaking roadways.

The buildings here, too, smack of naturalistic sensibilities. The chapel and crematory, designed by William Carbys Zimmerman, are primarily English Gothic in feel, but one look will reveal evidence of a Prairie School influence as well.

A name-dropper's paradise, Oak Woods has collected an astounding array of notables, including **Enrico Fermi** (1901-1954); **Jesse Binga** (1865-1950), the city's first black banker; Mob heavyweight **Giacomo "Big Jim" Colosimo** (d. 1920); the **parents of General John J. Pershing**; and **Mayor Harold Washington** (1922-1987), whose grave brings weekly visits by an anonymous, red rose-toting devotee.

The son of a Protestant minister and Democratic ward lead-

As one of the oldest cemeteries in the area, Oak Woods contains many monuments like these old limestone columns where the writing is no longer visible (*above*). The obelisk commemorating William Hale Thompson, 1920s Mayor of Chicago, also known as "Big Bill" and "Kaiser Bill" (*below left*). According to one political opponent, "The worst you can say of him is that he's stupid." The Confederate monument at Oak Woods marks the largest Confederate burial site in the North (below right) . An estimated 6,000 soldiers and sailors of the Confederacy are buried in concentric trenches around this monument, which was dedicated in 1895.

er, Washington ingeniously employed these seemingly conflicting roots to win the mayoral seat. Appealing to voters of the poor black wards that had traditionally backed the Democratic machine, Washington ran a campaign that was not only well-organized and financially stable, but rich with the religious gestures and symbolism common to black politics. The combination was a winner, and Harold Washington became the first black mayor in Chicago history.

The tallest monument in Oak Woods marks the grave of notorious Capone crony **"Big" Bill Thompson** (1867-1944), mayor of Chicago from 1915 to 1923 and again from 1927 to 1931. Though Thompson was quite a character while in office, his strangeness really shone between his mayoral stints: when his campaign went bad in 1923, Bill withdrew from the race, announcing his plan to sail to the South Seas on an expedition to find tree-climbing fish. But by the time his yacht, *Big Bill*, docked in New Orleans, Thompson had already abandoned ship.

While paying homage to the Mob-loving former mayor, crime buffs—and accountants—will want to visit the grave of another self-made Chicagoan: **Jake "Greasy Thumb" Guzik** (1887-1956), bookkeeper to Al Capone.

A treasure trove for Civil War enthusiasts, Oak Woods also hosts plots purchased by the **Grand Army of the Republic**, the **Chicago Veterans Association**, and the **Soldiers' Home**, among others. Yet the focal point among Oak Woods' many Civil War memorials remains **The Confederate Mound**. Burial site of some 6,000 Confederate soldiers, the mound holds the victims of Camp Douglas, a south side POW camp, and retains the distinction as the largest Northern burial site for Southern soldiers. In 1911, the names of over 4,000 of the POWs were inscribed on bronze plaques and affixed to the base of the enormous monument, the likeness of a Confederate infantryman towering 40 feet over its foundation.

More than military heroes rest here at Oak Woods. Civil rights activist **Ida B. Wells** (1862-1931) was buried here after a lifetime of fighting for the liberty of black Americans. Born of Mississippi slaves during the Civil War, Wells lost both parents and three siblings to yellow fever when she was only 14.

The simple headstone of Nobel laureate and atomic pioneer Enrico Fermi (*above*). Disassembled train parts, reproduced in limestone, honor railroad engineer Gale Cramer (*below*). On July 27, 1887, while piloting a passenger train near York, Indiana, Cramer saw another train approaching in the opposite direction on the same tracks. Although he could have dived for safety, he stayed at his post, applying the brakes and releasing steam. The train was slowed enough that Cramer was the only person killed in the collision. The monument was erected by the passengers whom he had saved.

Undaunted, Wells went on to college, becoming a teacher, writer, and lecturer, leading a national campaign against lynching and marching in black suffrage parades in several major cities. In Chicago, Wells founded the first black woman's club; years later, she consolidated seven of such clubs into the National Association of Colored Women's Clubs. During the first years of the 20th century, the reformer established the Negro Fellowship League to serve the everyday needs of the city's poorest blacks. The organization operated for ten years, often on Wells's own money. Ida continued to crusade until her death in 1931 and remained ardently outspoken, believing that the National Association for the Advancement of Colored People (NAACP) was far too meek in its mission.

Italian immigrant and pioneering physicist **Enrico Fermi** (1901-1954) was awarded the 1938 Nobel Prize in physics for his work with radioactivity. He is remembered best for his creation of the first self-sustaining nuclear chain reaction, an event which occurred at the University of Chicago in 1942 in a stopgap laboratory erected on the squash courts under the Stagg Field stands.

Fermi went on to Los Alamos to work as part of the team appointed to develop an atomic bomb. He later contributed to the development of the hydrogen bomb as well, but eventually opposed its development on ethical grounds. Fermi is buried at Oak Woods, not far from the University of Chicago.

Though local and national history buffs find Oak Woods intriguing, the site also appeals to a wide variety of other visitors, from train spotters to architecture buffs and nearly everyone in between.

Especially poignant is the monument commemorating the selfless courage of **Gale Cramer** (1850-1887), the engineer who gave his life for his train's passengers, whose grave is marked by a replica of that last train he drove.

Architecture students and buffs visit the limestone monument to **George A. Fuller** (d. 1900), who invented the modern contracting system for building construction and whose firm built Chicago's Rookery and Monadnock buildings and the Flatiron Building in New York City.

The grave of "Cap" Anson, manager of the Chicago White Stockings,
features a baseball and two bats (*above*). Runner Jesse Owens,
an African-American, embarrassed Hitler in the 1936 Berlin
Olympics by spectacularly disproving the Nazi ideas of Aryan
superiority. He is also buried at Oak Woods (*below*).

Sports fans will get a kick out of the crossed baseball bats marking the grave of Hall of Fame ballplayer **Adrian "Cap" Anson** (1852-1922), who also managed the Chicago White Stockings before they became the Cubs. Also at Oak Woods is the grave of Olympian **Jesse Owens** (1913-1980), who took the 1936 Berlin games by storm, winning four gold medals and breaking three world records. Ironically, Owens spent much of his later life smoking like a fiend and eventually died of lung cancer.

Unfortunately, Oak Woods' **Eternal Light** monument loses much of its effect to daylight-only visitation hours. The granite tower of this Holocaust memorial contains radioactive material that absorbs solar rays during the day, letting off a mystical light in the evening.

Near the southern wall of Oak Woods is a Jewish cemetery, similar in appearance to Chicago's other 19th-century Jewish cemeteries; monuments are densely packed together without space between the graves.

Plots are small and monuments close together in the Jewish sections of Oak Woods, which are located along the cemetery's south wall.

The monument to the Loretto Nuns at Mount Olivet is a
crucifix in the rather unusual form of a Celtic cross.
Originally one of the south side's major Catholic cemeteries,
both Italian and Irish roots run deep at Mount Olivet.

MOUNT OLIVET CEMETERY

2755 West 111th Street
Chicago
773/238-4435
Catholic, Est. 1885

Catherine O'Leary (d. 1895, age 68), as in *Mrs.* O'Leary, was recently and officially thanked by the city for letting her cow burn down the town in 1871. The mayor and other fans of post -fire Chicago credit the Great Conflagration with furnishing a clean slate for the city's ingenious planners. The heroic O'Leary is buried in this well-designed cemetery.

Established by Chicago's south side Irish in 1885, Mt. Olivet was the first of the south side Catholic cemeteries. Purchased

Two soldiers, faithfully reproduced in limestone, stand watch over adjacent lots in Mt. Olivet. McAuliffe, on the left, was killed during the Spanish-American War; his eternal companion, Carey, died in World War I.

under the guidance of Archbishop Patrick Feehan a year before its opening, the expanse instantly provided a more geographically practical alternative to burial at Calvary, far north in suburban Evanston.

In addition to the O'Leary plot, other Celtic highlights at Mt. Olivet include the **Irish Nationalist Society** obelisk and an 1897 monument to the **Ancient Order of Hibernians**. Designed by sculptor John Moore and financed by fund-raising picnics, the latter structure is a 30-foot tower embellished with traditional symbols: a wolfhound, a harp, and a Celtic cross. An unusual Roman brick mausoleum can also be found here.

The unusual obelisk of The Ancient Order of Hibernians—a burial society that provided graves for its members.

Still in place, too, at Mt. Olivet is the monument marking the original grave of **Alphonse "Al" Capone** (1899-1947), whose body was moved to Mt. Carmel Cemetery in Hillside because of the family's fear of grave robbers.

MOUNT GREENWOOD CEMETERY

2900 West 111th
Chicago
773/779-7417

Mount Greenwood, an aptly-named haven, is a woodsy refuge at the Chicago border. Lemont limestone-spotters will want to duck inside for a look at the chapel of this rolling Victorian retreat.

This Corinthian column holds aloft a tripod and sculpted flame; Masonic symbols decorate the base (*above*). A white bronze elk stands over the graves of members of the Benevolent Protective Order of Elks (*below*).

Material Considerations

Almost as diverse as the contents of the graves they mark are the elements used in the creation of funerary monuments.

Early in the history of the Midwest, limestone was the preferred medium. Quarried in a number of areas, Bedford, Indiana limestone offered the greatest ease of carving, and sculptors often demanded it. In Chicago and environs, the limestone quarried in Lemont, southwest of the city limits, found its way to the graves of thousands, its buttery hue and rough grain still easily distinguishable from the sleek granite and marble creations of later days. Lemont limestone was favored by architects as well, whose preferences are evidenced in the Chicago Water Tower and Pumping Station and in the elaborately arched and castellated entry gates of a number of area burial grounds. Some Chicago residents believe that the reported haunting of a number of local graves and cemeteries has something to do with the Lemont limestone used in their monuments and entry gates. Such believers hint at the existence of a special energy or other conductive quality inherent in the stone. Coincidence, however, seems a likelier explanation.

When limestone was beyond geographical or financial reach, other media were considered; namely, wood or wrought iron, which were often fashioned into fences that ran, decoratively and protectively, around gravesites. Sandstone, slate, and marble were also used, though granite was and is the most durable of monument materials.

Adding to the array were local foundries, which were sometimes commissioned to create bronze detailing or portraiture for the embellishment of tombs. A more affordable alternative was pot metal, which was used in the design of an increasing number of monuments. Later, some designers discovered concrete, which could be enhanced considerably by pressing seashells, colored glass, stones, or broken tiles into the fresh pouring.

ST. CASIMIR CEMETERY
4401 West 111th Street
Chicago
773/239-4422
Catholic, Est. 1903

This stunning Roman Catholic Lithuanian cemetery is perhaps the most artistically progressive in the Chicago area. Though the earlier graves are marked by typically Catholic stones and monuments, the markers over post-World War II plots are both huge and sensationally unconventional, combining novel images with unexpected materials, such as fiberglass and steel, to create singular and often pleasing effects. Spacing, too, is unusual at St. Casimir's: the ample, manicured lots provide plenty of breathing room for the exquisite monuments, resulting in the overall effect of a sculpture garden.

This white marble angel is a brilliant contrast to the dull grey granite of the cross and stairs behind.

METRO SOUTH

Broken stone curbing surrounds a plot near the fence in the abandoned
south suburban Bachelors Grove Cemetery, considered by some to be one
of the most haunted places in the United States, if not the world.

A vine-covered mausoleum in an older section of Resurrection Cemetery (*left*). The main gate of Resurrection Cemetery (*below*), where the ghost known as "Resurrection Mary" is alleged to have bent the bronze bars.

RESURRECTION CEMETERY

7201 South Archer Avenue
Justice
708/458-4770
Catholic, 1904

The Queen of Heaven in her glory, surrounded by cherubs. The statue is of white marble and stands atop a red granite base.

Search all you want for the most famous grave at this enormous graveyard just southwest of Chicago in the village of Justice. The free-wheeling phantom known as **Resurrection Mary** has been traced to a half dozen occupants of this cemetery, all young accident victims buried in the 1930s, and all named Mary. The easily frustrated may opt instead to examine the front gates on Archer Avenue. In the 1970s, a young woman clutching the bars from the inside was seen by a passing motorist. The driver called the police, who found no one trapped in the cemetery; however, the bars had been bent apart and seared with the imprint of two small hands. Though the cemetery administration had the bars removed and repaired, it is said that the damaged areas will not take paint. Folklore, perhaps, and yet the bars do bear two discolored strips of metal that remain to nag the skeptical, as do the testimonies of dozens of local residents who visited the site after the bizarre incident, claiming to have seen the unmistakable handprints with their own eyes.

This relatively modern cemetery has two mausoleums, a giant traditional structure and a garden variety one. Also buried here is former major league outfielder, **John Ostrowski**, who played for both the Cubs (1943-1946) and the White Sox (1949-1950).

BETHANIA CEMETERY

7701 South Archer Avenue
Justice
708/458-2270
Protestant, Est. 1894

Adjacent to Resurrection is this Protestant cemetery, its many German inscriptions revealing the heritage of the interred. A highlight of Bethania is the **Kathmann Monument** near the entrance. This intricately detailed stone, depicting a woman kneeling before a well, is expertly carved and exceptionally well preserved.

This forest scene, carved in relief on the side of Bethania's Kathmann monument (*above*), features a woman gazing into a well. (B*elow*) A statue of a woman descending stairs between a pair of bronze torches.

LITHUANIAN NATIONAL CEMETERY

8201 South Kean Road
Justice
708/458-0638
Protestant, Est. 1911

T his fiercely patriotic site boasts monuments to several Lithuanian presidents, burials of many area immigrants, and a constant scattering of gold, green, and red flags.

Secluded and serene, the cemetery is also home to the curious memorial commemorating the life of **Albert Vaitis Carter** (1915-1987). Born on the fourth of July, the eccentric Carter would celebrate his birthday in historic places like Plymouth Rock and Gettysburg—and ten separate towns named Independence. His monument bears witness to Carter's self-conscious achievements: all four sides of the stone are inscribed with details of his life's activities, from his occupation as *PERCUSSIONIST—DRUMMER TO YOU*, to the historic trails he traveled, to the events and attractions at which he was the first paying customer, among them, the Gateway Arch in St. Louis and Chicago's Sears Tower. Carter is no restless spirit, however. Though his gravestone attests to the fact that he *ENJOYED LIVING, AND IT WAS CONTAGIOUS*, it also makes perfectly clear that the buoyant wayfarer is now *AT REST— FINALLY.*

Albert Vaitis Carter, a drummer and collector of "firsts," is at rest—"finally." All four sides of his monument are inscribed with lists of his accomplishments and historic events he attended.

One of several cenotaphs, monuments to those buried elsewhere, in Chicagoland cemeteries, this one honors Lithuanian president Dr. Kazys Grinius (*left*). A woman clutches a bouquet of roses atop the Sudintas monument in Lithuanian National Cemetery (*below left*). Next to her is a broken column, symbolizing the end of a life. (*Below right*) This small cemetery is filled with statues such as this one, and those featuring porcelain photographs of the dead.

ARCHER WOODS CEMETERY
Kean Road & 84th Street
Justice

One of two Kean Road cemeteries, Archer Woods is known as the unsettling burial ground next to Lithuanian National Cemetery.

With good reason.

Visitors to this enclosure, set in a forested area off the main thoroughfares, are often uncomfortably treated to the sight of concrete burial vaults stacked up by the side of the road. Adding to the effect is the local legend of a weeping woman said to haunt Archer Woods, as well as old-timers' memories of the honky-tonk bars that used to stand along Kean Road.

Despite the negative popular impression, the rustic feel and varied markers of Archer Woods offers a pleasant tour.

EVERGREEN CEMETERY
8700 South Kedzie Avenue
Evergreen Park
773/776-8434

This sprawling Evergreen Park ossuary provides repose for a number of cultural groups, including Greeks, Ukrainians, Palestinians, and Jews.

A favorite destination is the grave of **Ray Schalk** (1892-1970), Chicago White Sox catcher and Hall of Famer.

ST. MARY CEMETERY
87th Street & Hamlin Avenue
Evergreen Park
708/422-8720
Catholic, Est. 1888

Several large Mexican-American sections have joined the earlier ethnic gatherings at this Evergreen Park site, established by south side Germans in 1888. Mourners of many cultures join to keep an enchanting grotto aglow with glimmering votives.

Two sports figures are buried here: popular Chicago Bears running back, **Brian Piccolo** (1943-1970), and **Edward C. Gaedel** (1925-1961), onetime midget baseball sensation.

Baseball showman Bill Veeck hired the diminutive athlete to play for the St. Louis Browns against the Detroit Tigers in the second game of a 1951 doubleheader. Between the games, the fun-loving Veeck had sponsored a 50th-anniversary extravaganza in honor of the American League, parading acrobats, antique cars, and a huge celebration cake—from which Gaedel emerged, sporting a Browns jersey bearing the number "1/8" and delighting the crowd.

Dismissing Gaedel as a charming stunt, fans went wild when he was announced as a pinch hitter in the second game's first inning. Unknown to even the umpires, Gaedel had actually been signed by the Browns several days earlier. Though Detroit's manager was infuriated, umpire Ed Hurley let Gaedel face the pitcher. Though he had been warned by Veeck against swinging, the 3-foot, 7-inch Gaedel couldn't resist. Reaching first base, Gaedel would recall he felt "like Babe Ruth."

After the game, enraged American League president Will Harridge had Gaedel's name removed from the records and, in a scathing letter to Bill Veeck, officially banned midgets from playing in future AL games.

CEDAR PARK CEMETERY
12540 South Halsted Street
Calumet Park
773/785-8840

T ucked between Blue Island and Chicago, this cozy Calumet Park cemetery serves both as the end of the road for race car driver **James L. Snyder** (1909-1939), and as home plate for Chicago White Sox infielder **Donald M. Kolloway, Sr.** (1918-1994).

LINCOLN CEMETERY
12300 South Kedzie Avenue
Blue Island
773/445-5400

O ne of two black cemeteries opened during Chicago's pre-World War I years in response to discriminatory policies of their white counterparts, Blue Island's Lincoln Cemetery was founded in 1911 by a cooperative organization supported by fraternal lodges.

Jazz immortals, **Lil Hardin Armstrong** (1898-1971), one of the most outstanding women of early jazz, and **Jimmy Reed** (1925-1976), whose guitar-embossed stone marks the resting place of "The Boss Man of the Blues," are buried at Lincoln.

Memphis-born Hardin was first invited to play with Sugar Johnny's Creole Orchestra while working as a pianist/demonstrator at a Chicago music store. She then went on to lead her own band at Chicago's Dreamland. In the 1920s, Hardin hooked up with King Oliver; there, in New Orleans, she met Louis Armstrong and became his second wife.

Some historians credit Hardin with the bulk of Armstrong's

success; she is often cited as the driving force behind his emergence as a great musician. Leaning on Louis to be more aggressive toward his own goals, Lil was a relentless, one-woman pep squad. It is said that, under her influence, Armstrong found the confidence to leave King Oliver's band and begin his own.

Lil maintained strong support of her husband's career, but she also followed her own star. Though she contributed greatly to some of Armstrong's Hot Five and Hot Seven recordings, Lil led a number of her own groups, including Lil's Hot Shots, and was featured in more than one Broadway production. After splitting with her husband in the late 1930s, Lil worked for Decca records as a swing vocalist and pianist, recording more than a dozen cuts before returning to Chicago and the nightclub circuit. She died while performing "St. Louis Blues," a month after Louis's death, at a memorial concert in Chicago.

Like Lil Hardin Armstrong, Jimmy Reed was a native Southerner. Born in Dunleith, Mississippi, the blues singer wrote his own songs, accompanying them with guitar and harmonica. As a teenager, Reed left school to find work, at first taking up farming jobs around the state. When World War II made Northern jobs more plentiful, he traveled to Chicago where he was promptly drafted into the Navy. After his discharge, he returned to Chicago to work in the steel mills and spent his free hours playing music with Willie Joe Duncan, who played the Diddley-bow (one-string guitar). But Reed's real joy was in playing with old friend, guitarist Eddie Taylor, a Dunleith chum who had also moved North for work.

In the mid 1950s, Reed scored a contract with VeeJay Records; his recording, "You Don't Have to Go" was a smash, and he followed it up with a string of hits, including "Ain't That Lovin' You Baby," "You Got Me Dizzy," "Big Boss Man," and "Bright Lights, Big City." Taylor added much to Reed's recordings, and together they put 14 hits on the R&B charts in the ten years after their debut.

Despite phenomenal success, Reed was plagued with problems. An epileptic and alcoholic, he constantly struggled for the physical stability necessary for his work. In later years, he became notorious for performing drunk, and his failing health led

Bessie Coleman was the first African-American woman to earn a pilot's license. The hand-tinted portrait affixed to her monument shows the young pilot standing before her plane.

to an early death in 1976 from respiratory failure.

Another Lincoln notable is **Bessie Coleman** (1892-1926). She is remembered primarily as the first African-American woman to gain a pilot's license, but went on to really soar as a stunt pilot.

Born in Texas in the early 1890s, Coleman's childhood was filled with helping her abandoned mother raise her 12 siblings. Picking cotton and doing laundry didn't leave much time for bettering herself, but Bessie had an unusual drive to achieve and dedicated her scarce free time to reading. Thanks to the traveling library that passed through her hometown of Atlanta on occasion, Coleman was able to finish high school and, with the aid of the money she made taking in washing, pay for a semester of college. Frustrated by her financial situation, Bessie did not abandon her quest for schooling, but turned to even "higher" education. Determined to become a pilot, she was turned away from every flying school she approached, because of both her race and her sex. Undiscouraged, Coleman appealed to an editor of the *Chicago Weekly Defender*, who helped her learn French, after which she obtained entrance to a French aviation school, paying her tuition with the money she made as a manicurist and working in a chili parlor. Bessie earned her pilot's license in

1921, two years before Amelia Earhart, becoming the only licensed black pilot in the world.

Progressing still further into aerobatics, Coleman received stunt training in Europe and then returned home to tour the United States, staging exhibition flights and lecturing on the promises of flight and racial progress. After five short years of stunt-flying, Coleman's World War I Jenny nose-dived during a barnstorming run in Florida; she was thrown from the plane and killed.

Another African-American pioneer rests at Lincoln: **Andrew "Rube" Foster** (1879-1930), eulogized upon his death in 1930 as the "father of Negro baseball."

Born in Texas in September of 1879, Foster began as a 17-year-old pitcher on the road with the Waco Yellow Jackets. His strong arm led him north to the mounds of some of the most successful black ball clubs of the time, among them the Philadelphia Giants and the Chicago Union Giants. He was given the nickname "Rube" after the pitcher Rube Waddell, whose Hall of Fame skill was bested by Foster at a 1902 exhibition game. The next year, fans cheered Foster through four straight wins of the so-called Colored World Series.

Foster's playing days laid the groundwork for his years of retirement from the game; he became a manager and entrepreneur, forming the Chicago American Giants in 1911 and going on to organize the Negro League in 1920, serving as its first president. Traveling in high style with his superstar Chicago team, Foster brought organized black baseball to an eager nation, and sensational fame to a black organization in a time when African-American celebrity was non-existent.

Despite a great and long career, Rube Foster could not elude the mental illness that overtook him in 1926, forcing him to quit baseball. After his death in an Illinois asylum four years later, he was mourned by millions who recognized early the pioneering spirit that, more than 50 years later, gained Foster election to the Baseball Hall of Fame.

OAK HILL CEMETERY
11900 South Kedzie Avenue
Blue Island
708/385-0132

This Blue Island site was founded by Scandinavians hailing from Chicago's south side. The vast acreage was originally designed for many years of service to the ethnic population of the surrounding area, but when Scandinavians began leaving the vicinity soon after the cemetery's founding, sections of the land were sold off for establishment as an African-American cemetery.

This monument (*above*) features a double-headed serpent entwined about itself. Oak Hill's community mausoleum evokes the grandeur of larger mausoleums (*below*).

MOUNT HOPE CEMETERY
115th Street & Fairfield Avenue
Blue Island
708/371-2818
Est. 1870s

A highlight of this 1870s Blue Island site is the **Rotary International Memorial**—a garden of bushes and burials surrounding a central monument to Chicagoan **Paul P. Harris** (1868-1947), the club's founder who settled in Chicago as a young man to study law.

Joining the business leaders at Mt. Hope is meat packer **Gustavus Swift** (1839-1903).

Civil War enthusiasts will appreciate the cemetery's lovely "white bronze" (zinc) statue of a Union soldier, erected by the Grand Army of the Republic.

And ballplayer **George D. "Buck" Weaver** (1890-1956) ducked out of the spotlight and into a plot here, after shaming himself as a member of the infamous 1919 Black Sox.

A row of hillside mausoleums at Mt. Hope (*above*). Such structures are relatively uncommon in the Chicago area, as most graveyards tend to be flat. (*Opposite page*) A white bronze (zinc) soldier of the Civil War, erected by the Grand Army of the Republic.

RESTVALE CEMETERY
117th Street & Laramie Avenue
Alsip
708/385-3506

Reminisce for a moment at the grave of **Nathaniel "Sweet-water" Clifton** (1926-1990), famed Harlem Globetrotter and DuSable High School basketball immortal. Or tour the plots of ten—count 'em—noted musicians, including the incomparable **Muddy Waters** (1915-1981).

Also at Restvale are blues buddies Samuel G. Maghett, otherwise known as **Magic Sam** (1936-1969), and King of the Blues Harmonica, **Walter Horton** (1918-1981).

And rounding out the cemetery's musical theme is a rare type of monument: an appropriately whimsical **stone organ**, just waiting for the ethereal fingers of Restvale's talented residents.

Visitors leaving Restvale should note the tiny adjacent cemetery known as **Hazel Green**, a site for local burials that dates from the late 19th century.

HOLY SEPULCHRE CEMETERY

6001 West 111th Street
Alsip
708/422-3020
Catholic, Est. 1923

After a remarkable life that included 21 years as Chicago mayor, quintessential machine politician **Richard J. Daley** (1902-1976) joined thousands of his constituents at this site, located along 111th Street in the nearby suburb of Alsip.

Leader of the Cook County Democratic party for 23 years and mayor for a whopping six terms, Daley evolved from figurehead of an organized, local force into a bona fide national

Richard J. Daley, Mayor of Chicago, is buried beneath a granite ledger bearing the seal of the city and the Prayer of St. Francis. Behind it is a Celtic cross.

presence, commanding the attention, and even subservience, of national political personalities.

Equally legendary dead or alive, the late Richard J. Daley continues to haunt the political life of his city, as well as the everyday life of his former neighbors. On the city's south side, Daley's lifelong home, a typical Chicago-style bungalow in the prototypical working-class neighborhood of Bridgeport, is still guarded 'round the clock by a squad car posted out front.

Despite Daley's sensational legacy, most of the crowds flocking to Holy Sepulchre are not seeking to honor "Hizzoner," but to say a silent prayer at the grave of an enigmatic little girl.

Mary Alice Quinn (1920-1935) died at the age of 14, after a short but intensely pious life of devotion. Following the example of Saint Theresa of Lisieux, who found the key to devotion in her

"Little Way" of everyday charity, Quinn won the faith and affection of scores of followers who believed her to have the stuff of sainthood. After her death, pilgrims gravitated to her gravesite, offer-

ing prayers, pleading for intercession in their needs, and even taking handfuls of soil as sacred souvenirs. In recognition of their faith, visitors are said to be treated to an overwhelming odor of roses, even in wintertime, a phenomenon reminiscent of St. Theresa's promise to send a "shower of roses" to assure the faithful of her constant intercession for them.

And torch singer **Helen Morgan** (1900-1941) took her final bow and exited to a plot here, after wooing the world with such famous cuts as "Can't Help Lovin' Dat Man," "Bill," "Frankie and Johnny," and other favorites.

Visitors to Holy Sepulchre will note the contrast between this cemetery's varied landscape and the overwhelmingly flat **Chapel Hill Gardens South**, directly across Central Avenue, whose burials are marked almost exclusively by flush stones.

The Mausoleum of the Archangels is a garden crypt, a new and increasingly popular method of interment with graves set into exterior walls, the space open to the environment.

BURR OAK CEMETERY
4400 West 127th Street
Alsip
773/233-5676

Harlem Globetrotter **Inman Jackson** (1907-1973) slam-dunked himself into a plot at this Alsip site, where he keeps heavenly company with another superstar.

After devouring seven husbands and an endless stream of alcohol and drugs, **Dinah Washington** (1924-1963), the self-styled "Queen of the Blues," laid herself down at Burr Oak at the age of 39. As a legend among the fans she left behind, however, she is as immortal as they come.

Born Ruth Jones in August of 1924, the Tuscaloosa, Alabama choir girl was hired by Lionel Hampton in 1943. Dinah sang with Hampton's band for three years, recording such smashes as "Evil Gal Blues" and "Salty Papa Blues."

After leaving the group, Washington turned to rhythm and blues, meeting with increased success and proving herself a versatile and talented artist. Later, her performances began to include hints of jazz, blues, and pop music, rounded out with favorite standards of the era. She also experimented with the new "soul" sound, becoming one of its most prominent early stars. Dinah recorded a string of hits in a number of vocal styles, including her most famous, "What a Difference a Day Makes."

Washington's broad appeal and obvious talent won her legions of fans and a fortune unknown to most black artists of the day. Reveling in her wealth, Dinah blossomed on a steady diet of jewels and furs, drugs and drinks—and men. As her career and confidence thrived, the beloved singer felt no need to ease up on her excess. At the age of 39, however, by all appearances content with both her public and personal lives, Dinah Washington died after overdosing on diet pills and liquor. She was buried with many tears at this suburban site.

Burr Oak bears the remains of two other jazz legends, **Willie**

Dixon (1915-1992) and **Otis Spann** (1930-1970).

A monumental presence at Chess Records, Dixon composed music, played bass on countless cuts, led the label's studio band, and arranged and produced the majority of the Chess blues blockbusters. After accompanying Chess on its way to major success, Dixon ducked out of the company to build up the new Cobra label on Chicago's west side. Cobra immediately took off after Dixon's work with Otis Rush ("I Can't Quit You, Baby"). Willie stayed on to bolster the fledgling careers of artists like Buddy Guy and Magic Sam. As the '60s dawned, however, financial discord sent Dixon back across town to grateful Chess.

Another Chess mainstay, pianist Spann distinguished himself in the 1960s as a solo artist. He is best remembered, however, as the man at the keyboard in the Muddy Waters Band.

Celebrity hounds will want to make one final visit—to the grave of actor **Lexie Bigham** (1968-1995), whose movie credits included *Boyz in the Hood, Dave, Seven, South Central,* and *High School High.*

ST. BENEDICT CEMETERY
4600 West 135th Street
Crestwood
773/238-3106
Catholic, Est. 1885

This modest site, managed by the office of Mount Olivet, shelters many members of the **Mantellate Sisters**, Servants of Mary, including **Reverend Mother Louis Pedrini** (1875-1938), founder of the order's American congregation.

BACHELORS GROVE CEMETERY
Rubio Woods Forest Preserve
143rd Street & the Midlothian Turnpike
Bremen Township, near Oak Forest, Midlothian, and Crestwood

This enigmatic site has been a thorn in the side of southwest suburban officials since the closing of the old Midlothian Turnpike in the 1960s, which barred the one-acre cemetery from vehicle traffic and simultaneously created the most legendary lovers lane in the metropolitan area.

Part of the Rubio Woods Forest Preserve, Bachelors Grove (also known as Batchelor Grove, Old Bachelor's Grove, Bachelder's Grove, Batchelor's Grove, English Bachelor's Grove, and others) was founded in the mid-19th century as Everdon's Cemetery, hosting its first burial when Eliza Scott was interred in November 1844. For many years a placid place where families picnicked on Sundays and fished in the site's quarry pond, the burial ground began its aesthetic decline in the 1950s and '60s, when teenagers enjoying the surrounding woods initiated reports

This gate is the entrance to Bachelor's Grove cemetery.
The chain-link fence has been ripped in several places.

of mysterious flashing lights and a "magic house" that would appear and disappear from a clearing in the forest.

Since these earliest reports of a haunted Bachelors Grove, myriad tales have taken root in the area's fertile soil, which is credited as the place of origin of a number of popular modern American folktales; for example, these woods are supposed to have been the site where the original "Hooked Maniac" of urban legend preyed on lovelorn victims after escaping from a mental institution. In addition, numerous other phantoms have joined the magic house in haunting the grove, including a two-headed man, a woman in white called "The Madonna of Bachelors Grove," ominous, darkly-hooded figures, and a man in a yellow suit who is reputed to appear and disappear in a shower of sparks.

Fueling the imaginative fire here are the ongoing reports of Satanic worship alleged to have occurred at Bachelors Grove since the 1960s. Far from unfounded, such reports were authenticated with some frequency during the '70s, when hooligans in search of kicks routinely dug up graves and rearranged tombstones, some leaving animal remains and other grisly tokens as calling cards.

Though Bachelors Grove is a heart-wrenching mess of a place these days, there is hope that local frustration at the continued ransacking of the site will inspire a renewed effort to restore to the cemetery some its former dignity.

Ceme-prairies
The Silver Lining of Abandonment

While cemetery lovers and survivors bemoan the declining state of ancient, local burial places, naturalists are urging the further under-maintenance of these often tiny, largely untended sites.

Increasingly, biologists are discovering that abandoned, or near-abandoned, cemetery grounds are sheltering rare plants and animals too often sacrificed to the strict landscaping rules proscribed by larger sites under centralized management. In Will County, scientists inspecting more than 150 "obsolete" graveyards have literally hit pay dirt time and again; a large number retain even their original soil structure. In addition, a number of endangered prairie species have been found flourishing within the untouched confines of these rural retreats.

Desperate to keep these treasures safe from the hands of well-meaning individuals and groups set on "cleaning up" their local cemeteries, several states, including Ohio, Indiana, and Illinois, have joined the nature conservancy in managing a number of local graveyards. Volunteers shun the mower, instead spending tedious hours hand-pulling overgrown grass and keeping trees in check with controlled fires.

Despite their loving attendance to these difficult duties, however, naturalists admit to being frustrated by one seemingly insurmountable obstacle: the unswerving determination of a minority of bereaved to keep the weeds off grandma's grave.

Originally settled in the early 1830s by British migrants from New England, a second influx of German settlers traveled to the Bachelors Grove area during the 1840s. Though local popular history traces the site's name to four single men who migrated to these woods during the first phase of settlement, resulting in the designation as "Bachelors" Grove, local researchers now believe that the true spelling of the place name was Batchelder, and that the Grove was named for the family that had settled in the area in 1845. Still, the popular name of Bachelors Grove persists, despite the more common historical use of the hybrid "Batchelor" Grove name, among others.

Though anywhere from 150 to 200 persons are estimated to have been buried in this tiny enclosure, fewer than 20 headstones remain. Fortunately, largely owing to the efforts of historian Brad L. Bettenhausen, a plat map was compiled in the mid-1990s, which was published along with background notes in the Fall 1995 issue of the South Suburban Genealogical and Historical Society's journal, *Where the Trails Cross*. Gathering research from area maps, students of Bremen High School, and members of local historical societies, Bettenhausen matched up burial records and plot locations to create a picture of the true Bachelors Grove, despite the vandalism, missing stones, and waist-high foliage of recent years. The result is an intriguing tale of settlement and growth and, sadly, of decline.

The last known burial of a body at Bachelors Grove took place in 1965; the last burial of ashes was recorded in 1989. Burials after 1950 are rare, and many remains have been disinterred and moved from Bachelors Grove throughout the century as a result of the migration of families, the need for larger plots, and, later, the horror of families at the desecration of the grounds. Still, a search for the origins of Blue Island should begin by walking the few hundred feet down the weed-choked road to the grove, where many of the area's earliest and most influential settlers have, in recent decades, endured a less than peaceful sleep.

Brought down by a storm, a dead tree adds to the desolate atmosphere of this accursed place.

St. James Church sits atop a small rise, surrounded by gravestones dating back to the 1830s (*above*). Retaining walls surround several plots in this very old graveyard built on uneven ground (*below*).

ST. JAMES CEMETERY
106th Street & Archer Avenue
Lemont
708/422-3020
Catholic, Est. 1837

More commonly known as St. James, The Sag, or simply St. James-Sag, this former Indian burial ground and French signal fort became a cemetery in 1837. Though St. Johannes Cemetery, one of the two burial sites at O'Hare International Airport, was also established that same year, burials at St. James-Sag were recorded before the official establishment of the cemetery, rendering it the Chicago area's oldest existing ossuary.

Located in Lemont Township, St. James-Sag takes its name both from the onsite Catholic church of St. James and for its location at Illinois Rte. 171 and the Calumet Sag Channel, but the church and its churchyard were established to serve Irish workers who dug another waterway, the Illinois and Michigan Canal, through the heavily wooded region along what is now Archer Avenue.

The construction of the I&M Canal provided a crucial link between the Great Lakes and the Illinois River, which had previously been separated by the so-called Chicago Portage, the low divide of prairie that frustrated explorers Marquette and Joliet in their travels north from the Mississippi via the Illinois and Des Plaines Rivers. In fact, it was Joliet who first introduced the idea of a canal, insisting that a minor one of only "half a league of prairie" would allow water traffic a clear shot from Lake Michigan to the Mississippi River and all points along its route. Ultimately, creating this crucial corridor would allow a much grander journey: a portage-free passage from New York to the Gulf of Mexico.

Joliet's vision went unheeded by the French Canadian government; preoccupied with the fur trade, officials viewed a potential canal as a superfluity, as did the British government which took control of the portage region after the French and Indian War. After the American Revolution, however, the establishment of military force became the priority, and the founding of Fort Dearborn, at the mouth of the Chicago River, began the trading boom that led to the re-emergence of talk about a canal. As always, talk was cheap. Though interest in a canal resurfaced in 1810, the necessary land was not secured for six more years, and it was another seven years before a Canal Commission was established by the state of Illinois.

A sorrowful woman stands near a cross decorated with a wreath of flowers.

The enormously slow pace of canal development kept steady. No money came to the commission, and the organization eventually folded. More than a decade passed before the forming of a new commission in 1835. Unlike its predecessor, the new body was empowered by the government to raise money toward its efforts and, finally, work on the Illinois & Michigan Canal was begun in the summer of 1836. The burst of energy and optimism that accompanied the onset of construction would prove short-lived, however. A relentless shortage of funding, made disastrous by the Panic of 1837, brought the sporadic work to an end in 1841. While the abandoned canal lay unfinished, investors were desperately sought by its commissioners, who struggled to secure funds from the east coast and even England. A full year later, the canalers took up their tools once more. At last, in 1848, 25 years after the establishment of the first Canal Commission, the locks were opened on the Illinois & Michigan Canal, and in April of that year, a cargo of sugar from New Orleans reached the docks at Buffalo, New York. American commerce would never be the same. Chicago itself was destined to become the very heart of that commerce, its population increasing an incredible 600 percent in the ten years after the dedication of the canal. But the success of the venture was not without a human cost.

The life of the canalers was often brutal, comprised of arduous, unsteady labor and uncertain and meager payment, underscored by a staggering communal disheartenment. Illness and death were among the inevitable by-products of the project, and a number of Irish-American canalers were laid to rest near the site of construction, in the churchyard of St. James.

This bluffside burial ground would prove infinitely superior to the two cemeteries that had been established in 1835 in Chicago proper. Both city sites were located on the very banks of the lake; as a result, upkeep of the plots was difficult to impossible, and the shallow graves often became unearthed. Though St. James was, and is, surrounded by countless rivers, canals, minor lakes, and sloughs, its steep and sloping layout has brought it through more than 160 years of service.

MOUNT GLENWOOD CEMETERY
18301 East Glenwood-Thornton Road
Glenwood
708/758-5663
Est. 1908

In prewar Chicago, as elsewhere, African-Americans attempting to form cooperative business ventures were usually in for disappointment. One of the only ways for a would-be business owner to gain any footing was by investing in a cemetery association. African-Americans were constantly frustrated by efforts to be assimilated into the white cemeteries. For example, the March 4, 1910 edition of the *Chicago Weekly Defender* said that one white cemetery was running an advertisement specifying their grounds "exclusively for the white race." And sliding price scales, adjusted according to the race of the customer, were so rampant among the white cemeteries that, in 1911, Edward Green, a black state legislator, pushed for passage of an amendment to the civil rights law forbidding lot sale discrimination.

While politicians like Green fought the good fight in their own arenas, black businessmen responded to discriminatory policies by founding cemeteries of their own. The first of these was Mt. Glenwood, which opened in 1908, and which heralded itself as the only Chicago cemetery with a non-discriminatory clause in its charter.

Perhaps the most popular site here at Mt. Glenwood is the grave of Robert Poole. Born in Sandersville, Georgia, Poole became one of the first followers of Wallace Fard, who used the teachings of the Jehovah's Witnesses to dismember the theology of the Trinity and fully humanize the figure of Jesus Christ. His theory of racism, in which the white race was created by an evil black god, sparked tremendous controversy, but won Fard some important converts. Poole was the most fervent.

The son of a Baptist minister, Fard eventually changed Robert's name to the Muslim name of Kariem. Several years after Poole's conversion, Fard disappeared, and some accused his apprentice of foul play, claiming that Poole had his teacher murdered to make way for Poole's own leadership.

Taking the helm of the movement, Poole changed his name to **Elijah Muhammad** (1897-1975) and went on to convert the boxer Cassius Clay (Muhammed Ali) and another preacher's son, Malcolm Little, who became Malcolm X.

Upon his death in 1975, Muhammad had headed the Nation of Islam for a full 40 years. Succeeding him was his son, Wallace D. Muhammad, who changed many of his father's doctrines to reflect a more orthodox Islam.

HOLY CROSS CEMETERY
801 Michigan City Road
Calumet City
708/862-5398
Catholic, Est. 1893

Legendary jazz drummer **Gene Krupa** (1909-1973) fidgets in his family plot at this Calumet City site.

A native Chicagoan, Krupa bought his first drum set with money earned from working as a window-washer and errand boy at south side Brown's Music Company. Though his passion for music eroded his grades, Krupa graduated high school and enrolled at Indiana's St. Joseph's College, where he studied under the classical guidance of Fr. Ildefonse Rapp. After less than a year of formal training, Krupa abandoned the classroom in favor of a career, spending the next years with commercial dance bands around Chicago. In the late '20s, Krupa found himself sitting through two musical shows a night at the local movie house, listening in rapt attention to a group of white jazz musicians called the Austin High Gang. It was the Gang's drummer, Dave Tough, who first took Krupa to see the legendary drummer, Baby Dodds. Krupa was instantly sold on black jazz,

An angel at Holy Cross Cemetery (*above*). Red granite
columns flank the door of this limestone mausoleum (*below*).
To one side are the words "What you are we were, what
we are now you will be. Think this over and go on."

nd he began modeling his own style on the patterns of Baby and other New Orleans drummers like Johnny Wells and Zutty Singleton. High on jam sessions with Bix Beiderbecke and Benny Goodman at the Three Deuces nightclub across from the Chicago Theater, Krupa finally recorded in 1927 with Austin High Gang members under the name of McKenzie-Condon's Chicagoans. The session proved pioneering when Krupa insisted on using his entire set, against the wishes of producer Tommy Rockwell. The resulting driving beat set the standard for the Chicago sound in jazz.

Krupa was soon impressing the greatest musicians of his time, including the Gershwins during his work with the orchestra for their Broadway hit, "Strike up the Band." He went on to dazzling performances with Benny Goodman and Tommy Dorsey. By the late 1940s, however, Krupa needed to save his career, threatened as it was by a 1943 arrest for marijuana possession. He set about re-forming his own orchestra, brilliantly incorporating trends of the fledgling bebop movement.

Gene Krupa died in 1973 in Yonkers, New York from heart failure during treatment for leukemia and emphysema. A requiem Mass was held at local St. Dennis Roman Catholic Church, and his body returned to the Chicago that had raised him.

A childlike angel clings to the cross while gazing upward.

IV. BURIALS
NOT IN
CEMETERIES

An iron gate in the base of this 35th-Street tomb opens to a
small room containing the sarcophagus of Senator Douglas.
The base of the sarcophagus reads "Teach my Children to
obey the Laws and uphold the Constitution."

The 96-foot monument to the "Little Giant" stands on what once was the Senator's 35th Street estate. The monument was designed by Leonard Wells Volk (see "Rosehill" chapter, p. 39) and features a statue of Senator Douglas at the top of the shaft. Around the base are four figures of women, representing History, Justice, Eloquence, and Illinois.

BURIALS OUTSIDE OF CEMETERIES

Aside from Ira Couch, whose Lincoln Park tomb still stands as it did when the area was City Cemetery, a number of other locals are interred in unconventional crannies, by choice or by circumstance.

One of the most notable is the tomb of **Stephen A. Douglas** (1813-1861), presidential opponent of Abraham Lincoln. The first state memorial to be erected in Illinois, the Douglas monument is the centerpiece of **Stephen A. Douglas Memorial Park** (35th Street & Lake Park Avenue, Chicago). Designed by renowned sculptor Leonard Volk, the structure boasts a larger-than-life-sized likeness of the "Little Giant." Douglas became a leading figure in the Illinois Democratic Party and went on to debate Abraham Lincoln during a bid for the Illinois Senate and then the presidential election of 1860. After being defeated, Douglas supported the new president, lecturing to the border states on Lincoln's behalf.

A 19th-century cemetery takes up a half-acre of **Yorktown Shopping Center**'s parking lot (Route 56/Butterfield Road & Highland Avenue, Lombard), having been established by William Boeger for the congregation of the Church of St. Paul, which once stood at Butterfield and Myers roads. Though the church closed its doors around the turn of the century, the cemetery remains, a pleasant peninsula in an ocean of automobiles.

Though his grave has been relocated, due in part to rampant vandalism, **Francis Stuyvesant Peabody** (1859-1922) continues to draw hundreds of teenagers a year to his Oak Brook estate, intrigued by the legends surrounding the late coal magnate.

When multimillionaire Peabody acquired nearly 850 acres of land in eastern Du Page County, he envisioned the site as an ideal home for him and his family. The resulting 39-room Tudor Gothic mansion emerged as the centerpiece of a lavish estate which included more than 12 acres of wetlands, nine acres of

Freeze!
A Chilling Alternative to Checking Out

If the high price of dying is getting you down, take heart: even in these days of outrageous funeral costs, burial is still a downright bargain—compared to the cost of sticking around. Cryonics providers, in the business of freezing folks at the moment of death in hopes of revival and survival in later, more medically advanced age, are currently charging about $125,000 for a full-body freeze, which includes indefinite storage at -320 degrees Fahrenheit in liquid nitrogen.

Though the fee seems whopping, it's rather necessary for business: only about 70 people are currently in cryonic suspension and these divided among four cryonics firms in California, Michigan, and Arizona. Combining business operating costs with freezing fees, and adding on the burden of storage for perhaps hundreds of years, cryonics companies could feasibly be called struggling. For these outfits, it is hoped another less expensive process will boost future income. Neurosuspension, the freezing of only the head (and storage in a cookpot of liquid nitrogen), is a relative steal; the going rate is a mere $60,000.

lakes and ponds, one-and-a-half acres of prairie, and nearly 70 acres of rolling lawns. Sadly, Peabody would not live to enjoy the site, which he christened **Mayslake** (Route 83 & 31st Street, Oak Brook) after his wife and daughter. Only three years after conceiving the project, Peabody was stricken with a heart attack while riding his horse on the estate grounds. Upon his death, Peabody's widow had her husband interred on the spot where he had died, and to mark the location she built over it a remarkable monument: the Portiuncula Chapel, an exact replica of the Chapel of St. Francis in Assisi, Italy.

The grieving Peabody family deserted the mansion after Francis's death, and in the spring of 1924, the estate was sold to the Franciscan Order, who built a retreat house next to the house and a friary elsewhere on the grounds. Some time after the change in title, the chapel was moved to its current location, facing Peabody's dream house.

Under cover of darkness, suburban curiosity-seekers have stolen upon the grounds of Mayslake for decades, undaunted by the monks who, until their move from the site in recent years, dealt with trespassers by apprehending them, taking them to the estate's little Portiuncula Chapel, and forcing them to pray through the night. The possibility of such punishment was worth the chance of finding the remains of the late Peabody, whose corpse was supposed to have been suspended in a glass casket filled with oil and interred somewhere on the estate.

Though Peabody's body was disinterred and relocated to one of the Archdiocesan cemeteries, the legend of Peabody's Tomb lives on, and there seems to be no end to the steady stream of believers determined to solve the Mayslake enigma.

Colonel Robert R. McCormick (1880-1955) rests on the grounds of his estate-turned-tourist attraction, **Cantigny** (1 South 151 Road, Wheaton). McCormick inherited the sprawling Red Oaks Farm from his grandfather, *Chicago Tribune* publisher Joseph Medill, who in the mid-1890s commissioned a country house from architect C.A. Collidge, designer of Chicago's Art Institute and public library. The resulting white frame colonial home was enlarged by McCormick in the 1930s, when he added a bedroom wing, sitting rooms, servants quarters and a new kitchen, an enormous library, and a private movie theater. By the time the building frenzy ended, Medill's 11-room country house had become a 35-room palace.

A World War I artillery officer in the First Division, McCormick renamed the estate Cantigny, after the Division's 1918 battle—America's first major victory of the conflict.

McCormick bequeathed the Cantigny estate to the people of Illinois; five years after his death in 1955, the War Memorial of the First Division was opened to the public. Each year, Cantigny plays host to more than 100,000 visitors to its renowned museum and spacious gardens, and for tours of the mansion and McCormick's placid garden tomb.

From **Clarence Darrow** (1857-1938) **Memorial Bridge**

(approx. 58th Street, east of Cornell Avenue) in Jackson Park behind the Museum of Science and Industry, one may gaze across the lagoon where the attorney's ashes were deposited and reflect on Darrow's figurative and literal enrichment of the city's environment.

And Cubs fans unknowingly visit the grave of musician **Steve Goodman** (1948-1984) during every home game: his ashes repose under **home plate at Wrigley Field** (Clark & Addison Streets, Chicago). A prolific songwriter and die-hard Cubs fan, Goodman wrote several songs for his favorite team, including "Go Cubs Go" and "A Dying Cubs Fan's Last Request." Yet, he is most remembered for his American classic, "The City of New Orleans," which won singer Arlo Guthrie much acclaim.

V. OUTLYING SITES

A lovely, aged monument at Union Ridge Cemetery
at 6700 West Higgins Road in Chicago.

OUTLYING SITES

Cemetery aficionados should note that in Illinois as in any state funerary intrigue extends outside the metropolitan area limits. The following are only a few of Illinois's many buried treasures.

Far south of the southernmost suburbs is the town of Metropolis whose **Masonic Cemetery** (R.R. #2) received the remains of **Robert Stroud** (1890-1963), the legendary "Birdman of Alcatraz." A pimp convicted for murder in Juneau, Alaska, Stroud was to spend 12 years imprisoned on McNeil Island for his crime, but was transferred to Leavenworth after attacking an orderly. There, just five years later, he stabbed a guard to death and was sentenced to be hanged. While he waited on death row, Stroud petitioned Mrs. Woodrow Wilson, begging for a lesser punishment. A week before his execution date, he was re-sentenced to life in prison.

With no chance of parole, Stroud had nothing but time, and he put it to good use. At Leavenworth, the convict had rescued a sickly bird, keeping it as a pet in his cell. Though this practice was not uncommon, Stroud's interest in his feathered friend grew into an obsession, and he eventually took in some 300 birds, caring for them in several cells that were allotted him by the prison administration. Far from an eccentric interest, Stroud's work with his birds was serious business. After engaging in formal research, the Birdman wrote two books: *Stroud's Digest on the Diseases of Birds* and *Diseases of Canaries.*

In 1942, Stroud was transferred to isolation in the notorious "D" block on Alcatraz, where his birds were barred. In these new surroundings, Stroud became sullen and angry, inspiring fellow inmates to frequent violence. After ten years, the Birdman decided on a new project; he began to write the story of his life. Remarkably, Stroud's manuscript was published only a year after its completion, and Hollywood went wild for the story.

Stroud never saw his story played out on the silver screen.

Like the chirping chums of his younger days, *The Birdman of Alcatraz*, with Burt Lancaster playing the title role, was banned from the infamous island, its subject left to a few more years of lonely reflection. He died in a prison hospital in 1963.

Yugoslavia's last king rests in a Libertyville sanctum: **St. Sava Orthodox Monastery** (32377 North Milwaukee Avenue), headquarters of the Serbian Orthodox Diocese of the U.S. and Canada. The 11-year-old **Peter II** took the throne in 1934, after the assassination of his father, Alexander I. Though he took official control six years later, he fled almost immediately afterward when the Germans invaded his kingdom and spent his self-imposed exile working at a savings and loan in California.

The grandson of Queen Victoria, Peter was destined to be buried with Victoria's own. When he died in 1970, however, the king was found to have specified in his will a burial at this Libertyville location, where he remains today, interred in the Monastery's onion-domed church.

St. Sava attracts a scattered population to its confines: Serbs from as far north as Milwaukee and as far south as Gary. Non-Serbs will find ample evidence of the site's ethnic heritage: like many Eastern European-Americans, St. Sava's Serbian visitors memorialize their dead with offerings of food and drink, left behind for the deceased after graveside picnics.

In the nearby town of Third Lake is another Serbian retreat: the **Monastery of the Most Holy Mother of God** (Route 45), also containing a cemetery. Picnic tables dot the gravesites marked by massive black stones inscribed with revolutionary quotations.

The **Elk Grove Cemetery** (under the off ramp for I-90 on Arlington Heights Road, Arlington Heights) boasts a wide range in age of markers, some dating to Colonial times. In fact, the cemetery shelters two veterans of the American Revolution.

Woodstock's **Oakland Cemetery** (Oakland Avenue & Jackson Street) cradles **Chester Gould** (1900-1985), creator of comic strip protagonist "Dick Tracy." Born in Pawnee, Oklahoma, Gould dreamed of being a cartoonist, an aspiration lavishly supported by his father, a newspaperman, who published his 7-year-old son's drawings in the *Pawnee Courier Dispatch*. After going to the Oklahoma Agricultural and Mechanical College, Gould headed to Chicago with 50 dollars in his pocket. Over the next ten years, he worked at every paper in the city except the *Post.* In 1921, he returned to school to rethink his career.

By 1931, Gould had decided he was a failure. Struggling to support his wife, Edna, and their daughter, Gould threw his last artistic energies into a clinging hope: to sell a comic strip to the *Chicago Tribune-New York News* syndicate. After trying to sell them literally hundreds of ideas, he despondently sent off a few frames chronicling the adventures of a down-to-earth crime-fighter called "Plainclothes Tracy." With Chicago in the grip of gangland rule, the concept of a heroic and honest detective proved golden. All *Tribune* publisher Joseph Medill required was a new name, and Gould furnished him with a beauty. Thus, "Dick" Tracy was born.

This Oak Hill Cemetery mausoleum has been sealed with a granite slab across the doorway, a common practice when an old mausoleum is filled to capacity and no further mourners are expected.

APPENDIX:
CHICAGO CEMETERIES

The following partial directory of Chicagoland cemeteries has been selectively compiled from lists belonging to the authors, the Wilbert Vault Company, the Catholic Cemeteries of Chicago, and *www.funeral.com*.

Acacia Park Cemetery
7800 Irving Park Road
Chicago

All Saints Cemetery
700 North River Road
Des Plaines

**All Saints Polish National
Catholic Cemetery**
9201 West Higgins Road
Chicago

Altenheim Cemetery
7824 Madison Street
Forest Park

Archer Woods Cemetery
Kean Road & 84th Street
Justice

Arlington Cemetery
Lake Street. & Frontage Road
Elmhurst

Ascension Cemetery
1920 Buckley Road
Libertyville

Assumption Cemetery
19500 South Cottage Grove
Glenwood

Assumption Cemetery
1 South 510 Winfield Road
Wheaton

Bachelors Grove Cemetery
Rubio Woods Forest Preserve
near Midlothian & Crestwood

Bethania Cemetery
7701 South Archer Avenue
Justice

Beth-El Cemetery
5736 North Pulaski Road
Chicago

Beverly Cemetery
Kedzie Avenue & 120th Street
Blue Island

**B'nai B'rith/
Mount Jehoshu Cemetery**
6600 West Addison Street
Chicago

Bohemian National Cemetery
5255 North Pulaski Road
Chicago

Bronswood Cemetery
3805 Madison Street
Oak Brook

Bulger Memorial Park
16th Street & Hirsch Terrace
Melrose Park

Burr Oak Cemetery
4400 West 127th Street
Alsip

Calvary Cemetery
301 Chicago Avenue
Evanston

Calvary Cemetery
Steger Road, near Western Avenue
Steger

Cantigny
1 South 151 Winfield Road
Wheaton

Cedar Park Cemetery
12540 South Halsted Street
Calumet Park

Chapel Hill Gardens, South
5501 West 111th Street
Worth

Chapel Hill Gardens, West
Route 83 & Roosevelt Road
Oak Brook Terrace

Christ Lutheran Cemetery
82nd Avenue & 147th Street
Orland Park

Church of the Holy Comforter
222 Kenilworth Avenue
Kenilworth

Clarence Darrow
Memorial Bridge
Jackson Park
58th Street, east of Cornell Avenue
Chicago

Clarendon Hills Cemetery
6900 South Cass Avenue
Darien

Concordia Cemetery
7900 Madison Street
Forest Park

Couch Mausoleum
Lincoln Park, behind the
Chicago Historical Society
Clark Street & North Avenue
Chicago

Douglas Memorial Park
35th Street & Lake Park Avenue
Chicago

Eden Memorial Park Cemetery
9851 West Irving Park Road
Schiller Park

Elk Grove Cemetery
Under the off ramp for I-90, on
Arlington Heights Road
Arlington Heights

Elm Lawn Cemetery
401 East Lake Street
Elmhurst

Elmwood Cemetery
2905 Thatcher Road
River Grove

Evergreen Cemetery
8700 South Kedzie Avenue
Evergreen Park

Evergreen Hill Memory Gardens
Richton Road & Park Avenue
Steger

Fairmount Willow Hills
Memorial Park Cemetery
9100 South Archer Avenue
Willow Springs

Fairview Memorial Park
Cemetery
900 North Wolf Road
Northlake

First Evangelical Lutheran
Cemetery
4135 West 127th Street
Alsip

Forest Home/
German Waldheim Cemetery
863 Desplaines Avenue
Forest Park

Fort Sheridan Cemetery
Fort Sheridan
East of Sheridan Road
Highwood

Free Sons of Israel Cemetery
1600 South Desplaines Avenue
Forest Park

Glen Oak Cemetery
4301 West Roosevelt Road
Hillside

Good Shepherd Cemetery
104th & 159 Streets
Orland Park

Graceland Cemetery
4001 North Clark Street
Chicago

Hazel Green Cemetery
115th Street & Laramie Avenue
Alsip

Highland Memorial Park
33100 North Hunt Club Road
Libertyville 60048

Hinsdale Animal Cemetery
6400 Bentley Avenue
Clarendon Hills

Holy Cross Cemetery
801 Michigan City Road
Calumet City

Holy Sepulchre Cemetery
6001 West 111th Street
Alsip

Homewood Memorial Gardens
600 West Ridge Road
Homewood

Immanual Cemetery
2317 South Wolf Road
Hillside

Irving Park Cemetery
7777 West Irving Park Road
Chicago

Jewish Graceland Cemetery
3919 North Clark Street
Chicago

Jewish Oak Ridge Cemetery
4301 West Oakridge Avenue
Hillside

Jewish Waldheim Cemetery
1800 South Harlem Avenue
Forest Park

Kenilworth Union Yard
211 Kenilworth Avenue
Kenilworth

Lincoln Cemetery
12300 South Kedzie Avenue
Blue Island

Lithuanian National Cemetery
8201 South Kean Avenue
Justice

Maryhill Cemetery
8600 North Milwaukee Avenue
Niles

Masonic Cemetery
R.R. #2
Metropolis

Mayslake
Route 83 & 31st Street
Oak Brook

Memorial Park Cemetery
9900 Gross Point Road
Skokie

Memory Gardens
2501 East Euclid Avenue
Arlington Heights

Menorah Gardens, Inc.
2630 South 17th Avenue
Broadview

**Monastery of the Most
Holy Mother of God**
Route 45
Third Lake

Montrose Cemetery
5400 North Pulaski Road
Chicago

Mount Auburn Memorial Park
4101 South Oak Park Avenue
Stickney

Mount Carmel Cemetery
1400 South Wolf Road
Hillside

Mount Emblem Cemetery
510 West Grand Avenue
Elmhurst

**Mount Glenwood
Memory Gardens, South**
18301 East Glenwood-Thornton
Road
Glenwood

**Mount Glenwood
Memory Gardens, West**
8301 South Kean Road
Willow Springs

Mount Greenwood Cemetery
2900 West 11th Street
Chicago

Mount Hope Cemetery
115th Street & Fairfield Avenue
Chicago

Mount Hope Cemetery
226 Orchard Street
Elgin

Mount Isaiah Israel Cemetery
3600 North Narragansett Avenue
Chicago

Mount Mayriv Cemetery
3600 North Narragansett Avenue
Chicago

Mount Olive Cemetery
3800 North Narragansett Avenue
Chicago

Mount Olivet Cemetery
2755 West 111th Street
Chicago

Mount Vernon Memorial Estates
119th Street & Archer Avenue
Lemont

New Light Cemetery
6807 North East Prairie Road
Lincolnwood

Northshore Garden of Memories
18th Street & Green Bay Road
North Chicago

Norwood Park Cemetery
6505 North Northwest Highway
Chicago

Oak Hill Cemetery
11900 South Kedzie Avenue
Blue Island

Oakland Cemetery
Oakland Avenue & Jackson Street
Woodstock

Oakland Memory Lanes
15200 Lincoln Avenue
Dolton

Oak Ridge Cemetery
4301 West Roosevelt Road
Hillside

Oak Woods Cemetery
1035 East 67th Street
Chicago

Our Lady of Sorrows Cemetery
1400 South Wolf Road
Hillside

Palos Oak Hill Cemetery
131st Street, 1 block east of
Southwest Highway
Palos Park 60464

Parkholm Cemetery
2501 La Grange Road
La Grange Park

Pine View Memorial Park
10750 West Beach Road
Waukegan

Queen of Heaven Cemetery
1400 South Wolf Road
Hillside

Randhill Park Cemetery
1700 West Rand Road
Arlington Heights

Rest Haven Cemetery
O'Hare International Airport
Chicago

Restvale Cemetery
117th Street & Laramie Avenue
Alsip

Resurrection Cemetery
7201 South Archer Avenue
Justice

Ridgelawn Cemetery
5736 North Pulaski Road
Chicago

Ridgewood Cemetery
9900 North Milwaukee Avenue
Des Plaines

**Robinson Woods
Indian Burial Ground**
Robinson Woods North
Lawrence Avenue &
East River Road
Chicago

Rosehill Cemetery
5800 North Ravenswood Avenue
Chicago

Rosemont Park Cemetery
6758 West Addison Street
Chicago

Sacred Heart Cemetery
Lee Road
Northbrook

Saint Adalbert Cemetery
6800 North Milwaukee Avenue
Niles

Saint Alphonsus Cemetery
State Street, north of Weimer
Lemont

**Saint Andrew's Ukrainian
Orthodox Cemetery**
300 East Army Trail Road
Bloomingdale

Saint Anne Cemetery
Sauk Trail & Westwood Drive
Park Forest

Saint Bede Cemetery
Wilson Road & Grand Avenue
Fox Lake

Saint Benedict Cemetery
4600 West 135th Street
Crestwood

Saint Boniface Cemetery
4901 North Clark Street
Chicago

Saint Casimir Cemetery
4401 West 111th Street
Chicago

Saint Gabriel Cemetery
164th Street & Cicero Avenue
Oak Forest

Saint Henry Cemetery
Devon & Ridge Avenues
Chicago

Saint James Cemetery
Calumet Expressway & Sauk Trail
Lemont

Saint James-Sag Cemetery
106th Street & Archer Avenue
Lemont

Saint John's Cemetery
3724 North Washington Street
Oak Brook

**Saint John's/Saint Johannes
Cemetery**
O' Hare International Airport
Chicago

Saint Joseph Cemetery
Belmont & Cumberland Avenues
River Grove

Saint Joseph Cemetery
Route 120, east of Fairfield Road
Round Lake

Saint Joseph Cemetery
Ridge Road & Lake Street
Wilmette

**Saint Luke/Saint Lucas
Cemetery**
5300 North Pulaski Road
Chicago

Saint Mark Cemetery
15W455 79th Street
Hinsdale

Saint Mary Cemetery
87th Street & Hamlin Avenue
Evergreen Park

Saint Mary Cemetery
Ridge Road
Highland Park

Saint Mary Cemetery
Sheridan Road & Spruce Avenue
Lake Forest

Saint Mary Cemetery
801 South Genesee Street
Waukegan

Saint Michael Cemetery
159th Street & Will Cook Road
Orland Park

**Saint Michael the Archangel
Cemetery**
1185 West Algonquin Road
Palatine

**Saint Nicholas
Ukrainian Cemetery**
8901 West Higgins Road
Chicago

Saint Patrick Cemetery
Telegraph Road, near Everett Road
Lake Forest

Saint Patrick Cemetery
Bluff Road
Lemont

Saint Peter Cemetery
8115 Niles Center Road
Skokie

Saint Sava Orthodox Monastery
32377 North Milwaukee Avenue
Libertyville

**Saints Cyril &
Methodius Cemetery**
State Street, south of
Keepataw Drive
Lemont

Shalom Memorial Park
1700 West Rand Road
Arlington Heights

Sunset Memorial Park
3100 Shermer Road
Northbrook

Town of Maine Cemetery
Dee Road & Touhy Avenue
Park Ridge

Transfiguration Cemetery
Route 176, east of Route 59
Wauconda

**Trinity Evangelical Lutheran
Cemetery**
6850 West 159th Street
Tinley Park

Union Ridge Cemetery
6700 West Higgins Road
Chicago

Van Zirngibl (Andreas) Grave
Illinois Steel Scrap Yard
9230 South Ewing Avenue
Chicago

Washington Memory Gardens
701 Ridge Road
Homewood

Westlawn Cemetery
7801 West Montrose Avenue
Chicago

White Cemetery
Cuba Road
Barrington

Woodlawn Cemetery
7600 West Cermak Road
Forest Park

Wrigley Field, Home Plate
Clark & Addison Streets
Chicago

Wunder's Cemetery
3963 North Clark Street
Chicago

Yorktown Shopping Center
Route 56/Butterfield Road
& Highland Avenue
Lombard

BIBLIOGRAPHY

CHICAGO GRAVEYARDS

Bohemian National Cemetery Association. *The Centennial of the Bohemian National Cemetery Association of Chicago, Illinois.* Berwyn, Illinois: Bohemian National Cemetery Association, 1977.

Historical Society of Oak Park and River Forest. *Nature's Choicest Spot: A Guide to Forest Home and German Waldheim Cemeteries.* Oak Park, Illinois: Historical Society of Oak Park and River Forest, 1998.

Hucke, Matt. "Graveyards of Chicago." *www.graveyards.com.*

Kezys, Algimantas, ed. *A Lithuanian Cemetery.* Chicago: Lithuanian Photo Library and Loyola University Press, 1976.

Lanctot, Barbara. *A Walk Through Graceland Cemetery.* Chicago: Chicago Architecture Foundation, 1988.

Mahany, Barbara. "Burial treasures: Joan Pomaranc's grave and glorious tales make cemeteries come alive." *Chicago Tribune,* 6 November 1991.

Wendell, David. *The Civil War at Rosehill.* Chicago: David Wendell, 1994.

GRAVEYARDS

Brown, John Gary. *Soul in the Stone: Cemetery Art From America's Heartland.* Lawrence: University Press of Kansas, 1994.

Jackson, Kenneth, and Camilo José Vergara. *Silent Cities: The Evolution of the American Cemetery.* New York: Princeton Architectural Press, 1989.

Keister, Douglas, and Xavier Cronin. *Going Out in Style: The Architecture of Eternity.* New York: Facts On File, Inc., 1997.

Kestenbaum, Larry. "The Political Graveyard." *www.politicalgraveyard.com.*

Krajick, Kevin. "Pushing Up Orchids." *Audubon*, vol. 100 (September-October 1998).

Robinson, David. *Beautiful Death: Art of the Cemetery.* New York: Penguin Books, 1996.

Stanton, Scott, and Robin Stanton. *The Tombstone Tourist: Musicians.* Portland, Oregon: 3T Publishing, 1998.

Tipton, Jim. "Find-A-Grave." *www.findagrave.com.*

"USGenWeb Archives: Cook County, Illinois." *www.rootsweb.com/~usgenweb/il/cook/cook.htm.*

DEATH AND FUNERAL CUSTOMS

Alger, Alexandra. "The New (and More Convenient) American Way of Death." *Fortune*, vol. 158 (Oct. 21, 1996).

Brown, Ed. "Would You Pay $125,000 to Get Frozen? The Uncertain Future of the Cryonic Suspension Industry." *Fortune*, vol. 136 (November 24, 1997).

Lamm, Maurice. *The Jewish Way in Death and Mourning.* New York: Jonathan David Publishers, 1972.

"World's Way of Death, The." *The Economist.* (Nov. 14, 1998).

SACRED SITES AND ESOTERIC SYMBOLISM

Yronwode, Cat. "Lucky Mojo Archive." *www.luckymojo.com.*

CHICAGO GHOSTS

Bielski, Ursula. *Chicago Haunts: Ghostly Lore of the Windy City.* Chicago: Lake Claremont Press, 1997.

Clearfield, Dylan. *Chicagoland Ghosts.* Holt, Michigan: Thunder Bay Press, 1997.

Taylor, Troy. *Haunted Illinois.* Alton, Illinois: Whitechapel Productions Press, 1999.

GHOSTS

Bingham, Joan, and Dolores Riccio. *More Haunted Houses.* Pocket Books, 1991.

Hauck, Dennis William. *Haunted Places, The National Directory.* Penguin Books, 1996.

Scott, Beth, and Michael Norman. *Haunted Heartland.* New York: Warner Books, 1985.

CHICAGO ARCHITECTURE

Commission on Chicago Historical and Architectural Landmarks. *Landmark Neighborhoods in Chicago.* Chicago: Commission on Chicago Historical and Architectural Landmarks, 1981.

Sinkevitch, Alice, ed. *AIA Guide to Chicago.* New York: Harcourt Brace & Company, 1993.

CHICAGO CRIME

Johnson, Curt, with R. Craig Sautter. *Wicked City, Chicago: From Kenna to Capone.* December Press, 1994.

Kobler, John. *Capone: The Life and World of Al Capone*. Da Capo Press, 1971.

Ness, Eliot, with Oscar Fraley. *The Untouchables*. Popular Library, 1957.

ETHNIC CHICAGO & IMMIGRATION HISTORY

Cutler, Irving. *The Jews of Chicago: From Shletl to Suburb*. Urbana: University of Illinois Press, 1996.

Hofmeister, Rudolf A. *The Germans of Chicago*. Champaign, Illinois: Stipes Publishing Company, 1976.

Lindberg, Richard. *Passport's Guide to Ethnic Chicago: A Complete Guide to the Many Faces and Cultures of Chicago*. Lincolnwood, Illinois: NTC Publishing Group, 1993.

Sclair, Helen A. "Ethnic Cemeteries: Underground Rites." In *Ethnic Chicago: A Multi-cultural Portrait*, ed. Melvin G. Holli and Peter D'A. Jones, 618-639. Wm. B. Eerdmans Publishing Co., 1995.

Spear, Allan H. *Black Chicago: The Making of a Negro Ghetto, 1890-1902*. Chicago: University of Chicago Press, 1967.

CHICAGO PERSONALITIES

Heise, Kenan, and Ed Baumann. *Chicago Originals: A Cast of the City's Colorful Characters*. Chicago: Bonus Books, 1995.

Holli, Melvin G. *The Mayors: The Chicago Political Tradition*. Carbondale: Southern Illinois University Press, 1995.

Royko, Mike. *Boss: Richard J. Daley of Chicago*. New York: E. P. Dutton and Company, 1971.

Sawyers, June Skinner. *Chicago Portraits*. Chicago: Loyola University Press, 1991.

CHICAGO HISTORY

Adelman, William J. *Haymarket Revisited.* Chicago: Illinois Labor
History Society, 1986.

Cowan, David and John Kuenster. *To Sleep With the Angels: The Story
of a Fire.* Chicago: Ivan R. Dee, 1996.

Heise, Kenan. *Is There Only One Chicago?* Westover Publishing
Company, 1973.

Kogan, Herman, and Lloyd Wendt. *Chicago: A Pictorial History.*
Bonanza Books, 1958.

Levy, George. *To Die in Chicago.* Evanston: Evanston Publishing Inc.,
1994.

Longstreet, Stephen. *Chicago 1860-1919.* New York: David McKay
Company, Inc., 1973.

Lowe, David. *Lost Chicago.* New York: American Legacy Press, 1975.

Wesolowski, Dr. Wayne E. "The Long Trip Home." *American History,*
vol. 30 (July 1995).

Winslow, Charles S. *Early Chicago.* Chicago: Charles S. Winslow, 1947.

TOURING CHICAGO

Hayner, Don, and Tom McNamee. *Chicago Sun-Times Metro Chicago
Almanac.* Chicago: Chicago Sun-Times and Bonus Books, 1993.

Heise, Kenan, and Mark Frazel. *Hands On Chicago: Getting Hold of the
City.* Chicago: Bonus Books, 1987.

Pohlen, Jerome. *Cool Spots, USA: Illinois.* Lincolnshire, Illinois: Jerome
Pohlen, 1995.

A favorite monument at St. Lucas/St. Luke Cemetery
at 5300 North Pulaski Road in Chicago.

INDEX

A

abandoned cemeteries
  Archer Woods, 167
  Bachelors Grove, 180-183
Acacia Park Cemetery, 91-93
Accardo, Antonio, 135-137
African-American cemeteries/
  sections
  Burr Oak, 178-179
  Lincoln, 169-172
  Mount Glenwood, 188-189
  Oak Hill, 173
  Restvale, 175
  Sunset Memorial Park, 76
Albanian cemeteries/sections
  Elmwood, 101
All Saints Cemetery, 77-78
All Saints Polish National Catholic
  Cemetery, 83
Altenheim Cemetery, 120
Altgeld, John Peter, 20
Ancient Order of Hibernians, 156
Anderson, Peirce, 29
Archbishop Feehan, 126
Archbishop Quigley, 126
Archer Woods Cemetery, 167
Arlington Cemetery, 122
Armenian cemeteries/sections
  Mount Olive, 95
Armour, Philip D., 15
Armstrong, George B., 45
Armstrong, Lil Hardin, 169-170
ashes, *see also* cremains, 57, 60,
  61, 76, 183, 198, 199

B

Bachelors Grove Cemetery, 180-183
Bangs, George S., 38
Battaglia, Sam, 134
Belushi, John, 101
Benevolent Protective Order of
  Elks, 157
Bernardin, Joseph Cardinal,
  125-126
Bethania Cemetery, 164
Beth-El Cemetery, 62
Bigham, Lexie, 179
Binga, Jesse, 147
Bishop Quarter, 126
Bishops Mausoleum, 125
Boerner, William, 86
Bohemian National Cemetery, 53-62
Boone, Levi Day, 45
Boyington, W.W., 37
Brickhouse, Jack, 48
Bulgarian cemeteries/sections
  Elmwood, 101
burial customs, 75-76
Burnett, Chester A., *see* Howlin'
  Wolf
Burnett, Leo, 38
Burnham, Daniel, 28
Burr Oak Cemetery, 178-179

C

Calvary Cemetery, 65-68
Cambodian cemeteries/sections
  Montrose, 52
Cambrian Society, 103

Cantigny, 198
Capone, Alphonse "Al", 127-128, 133-134, 136, 149, 156
Caray, Harry, 78
Carter, Albert Vaitis, 165
Catholic cemeteries
   All Saints, 77-78
   Calvary, 65-68
   Holy Cross, 189-191
   Holy Sepulchre, 176-177
   Mount Carmel, 125-133
   Queen of Heaven, 134-140
   Resurrection, 163-164
   St. Adalbert, 71-74
   St. Benedict, 179
   St. Boniface, 34-36
   St. Casimir, 159
   St. Henry, 49-52
   St. James-Sag, 184-187
   St. Joseph, 99-100
   St. Mary, 168
Cedar Park Cemetery, 169-172
Chicago City Cemetery, 11-12
Chicago Veterans Association, 149
Chinese cemeteries/sections
   Mount Auburn, 120
Church of the Holy Comforter, 69
cemeteries, abandoned, see abandoned cemeteries
cemeteries, ethnic, see ethnic cemeteries
cemeteries, Catholic, see Catholic cemeteries
cemeteries, Jewish, see Jewish cemeteries
cemeteries, Masonic, see Masonic cemeteries
cemeteries, pet, see pet cemeteries
cemeteries, Protestant, see Protestant cemeteries
cenotaphs, 34-35, 101, 166
Cermak, Mayor Anton, 55-56
Cigar Makers International Union, 109
City Cemetery, 11-12
Civil War monuments, 35, 47, 57-58, 60, 63, 65, 149, 174
Civil War Veterans Monument, 57, 60
Clarence Darrow Memorial Bridge, 198
Clarke, Inez, 24
Clifton, Nathaniel "Sweetwater", 175
Cody, Joseph Cardinal, 126
Coleman, Bessie, 171-172
Colonel Mulligan, 65
Colosimo, Giacomo "Big Jim", 127, 146-147
columbariums, 58, 60, 62
Colvin, Harvey Doolittle, 45
Comiskey, Charles, 67
Concordia Cemetery, 118-119
Confederate Mound, The, 149
Congregation of the Sons of Peace, 32
Cook County Poor Farm and Insane Asylum, 87
Couch, Ira, 11
Cramer, Gale, 151
Cregier, DeWitt Clinton, 45
cremains, 60-61
cremation, 61, 73, 75
Cremation Society of North America, 61
crematoriums, 13, 52, 57, 58, 70, 147
cryonics, 196
Cudahy, John, 65
Cummings, Edmund, 111
Czech cemeteries/sections
   Bohemian National, 53-62
   Mount Auburn, 120
   St. Adalbert, 71-74
   Woodlawn, 117-118

D

Daley, Richard J., 176
Darrow, Clarence, 198
Dawes, Charles Gates, 38
DeLucia, Felice, *see* Ricca, Paul
  "The Waiter"
DeMora, Angelo, 132
DeMora, James Vincenzo, *see*
  McGurn, "Machine Gun Jack"
Dick, A.B., 38
Di Salvo Family, the, 131
Dixon, Willie, 179
Douglas, Stephen A., 195
Douglas Tomb, 195
Dreschler, Charles, 111
Dreschler, Sophy Sievert, 111
Dunne, Edward F., 65, 67
Dusak, Ervin, 118

E

Eappen, Matthew, 77
Eastland Disaster, 55, 118
Eichenbaum Monument, 62
Elfring, Laura, 86
Elk Grove Cemetery, 202
Elm Lawn Cemetery, 121
Elmwood Cemetery, 101
ethnic cemeteries/cemetery
  sections
  African-American, 76, 169-172,
    173, 175, 178-179, 188-189
  Albanian, 101
  Armenian, 95
  Bulgarian, 101
  Cambodian, 52
  Chinese, 120
  Czech, 53-62, 71-74, 117-118,
    120
  German, 33, 34-36, 49-52, 99-
    100, 101, 102-111, 118-119,

120, 164, 168
  Greek, 101, 167
  Gypsy, 52, 101, 102-111
  Hispanic, 49, 52, 168
  Indian, 52
  Iranian, 52
  Irish, 65-68, 77, 154-156, 176-
    177, 184-187
  Italian, 125-133, 134-140, 154-
    156
  Japanese, 52
  Jewish, 30-32, 37, 62, 78, 95,
    112-116, 153, 167
  Latvian, 95
  Lithuanian, 159, 165-166
  Luxembourger, 49-52
  Macedonian, 101
  Mexican, 52, 168
  Native American, 88
  Palestinian, 167
  Polish, 71-74, 83, 163-164, 189-
    191
  Puerto Rican, 52
  Russian, 101
  Scandinavian, 94-95, 101, 173
  Serbian, 52, 202
  Ukrainian, 83. 101, 167
  Welsh, 103
Enrico, Fermi, 147, 150-151
Eternal Light Monument, 153
Evergreen Cemetery, 167

F

Farrell, James T., 68
Fellows, Lulu, 2, 48
Field, Eugene, 69
Field, Marshall, 14
Field of Honor, 104
Figg, Bob, 67
Fitzsimmons, Robert, 25
Florsheim, Milton, 39, 42

Forest Home Cemetery, 102-11
forest preserves, 88
Fort Sheridan Cemetery, 69
Foster, Andrew "Rube", 172
Franks, Bobby, 45, 48
Fraske, Fredrak, 74
Fuller, George A., 151
Fuller, Melville, 23

G

Gaedel, Edward C., 168
Gale, Edwin, 111
Garrett, Augustus, 45
Genna Family, the, 128, 132
German cemeteries/sections
  Altenheim, 120
  Bethania, 164
  Concordia, 118-119
  Elmwood, 101
  Forest Home/German Waldheim,
    102-111
  St. Boniface, 34-36
  St. Henry, 49-52
  St. Joseph, 99-100
  St. Mary, 168
  Wunder's, 33
German Waldheim Cemetery, 102-
  11
Getty, Henry Harrison, 27
Giancana, Sam "Mooney", 133, 136
Gill, Flora, 111
Gillis, Lester, see Nelson, "Baby
  Face"
Goldman, Emma, 105
Goodman Family, The, 15,19
Goodman, Steve, 198-199
Goodrich Family, the, 38
Gould, Chester, 202-203
Graceland Cemetery, 13-29
Grand Army of the Republic
  Forest Home, 103-104

Oak Woods, 149
Graves, Dexter, 22
Gray, Harold Lincoln, 123
Great Chicago Fire, The, 19
Greek cemeteries/sections
  Elmwood, 101
  Evergreen, 167
Griffin, Marion Mahony, 27
Grinius, Dr. Kazys, 166
Grunow Family, the, 110
Gusenberg, Frank, 94
Gusenberg, Peter, 94
Guzik, Jake "Greasy Thumb", 149
Gypsy cemeteries/sections
  Elmwood, 101
  Forest Home, 102-111
  Montrose, 52

H

Haase, Ferdinand, 102-103, 111
Hackett, John, 69
Halas, George Jr., 77
Halas, George "Papa Bear", 74
Harridge, Will, 70
Harris Family, the, 38
Harris, Paul P., 174
Harrison, Carter Henry, 24
Harrison, Carter Henry II, 24
Hartnett, Charles "Gabby", 77
Haymarket Martyrs' Monument,
  104-105
Hemingway, Clarence, 109
Hemingway, Grace, 109
Hines, Edward, 65
Hinkley, Otis Ward, 38
Hinsdale Animal Cemetery, 141
Hispanic Cemeteries/sections
  Montrose, 52
  St. Henry, 49
  St. Mary, 168
Holy Cross Cemetery, 189-191

Holy Name Cathedral, 125
Holy Sepulchre Cemetery, 176-177
Hopkins, John P., 67
Horatio N. May Chapel, 47
Horton, Walter, 175
Howlin' Wolf, 123-124
Hulbert, William A., 25
Hull, Charles, 38
Humphrey, Doris, 109
Hyman Family, the, 32

I

Independent Order of Odd Fellows,
  109
Indian cemeteries/sections
  Montrose, 52
International Alliance of Bill
  Posters and Billers, 109
Iranian cemeteries/sections
  Montrose, 52
Irish cemeteries/sections
  All Saints, 77-78
  Calvary, 65-68
  Holy Sepulchre, 176-177
  Mount Olivet, 154-156
  St. James-Sag, 184-187
Irish National Society, 156
Iroquois Theatre Fire Memorial, 52
Irving Park Cemetery, 94
Italian cemeteries/sections
  Mount Carmel, 125-133
  Mount Olivet, 154-156
  Queen of Heaven, 134-140

J

Jackson, Inman, 178
Jackson Park, 198
Japanese cemeteries/sections
  Montrose, 51-52

Japanese Mutual Aid Society, 50-51
Jenney, William Le Baron, 29
Jewish cemeteries/sections
  Beth-El, 62
  Evergreen, 167
  Jewish Graceland, 30-32
  Jewish Waldheim, 112-116
  Mount B'nai B'rith, 95
  Mount Isaiah, 95
  Mount Mayriv, 95
  Oak Woods, 53
  Ridgelawn, 62
  Rosemont Park, 95
  Rosehill, 37
  Shalom Memorial Park, 78
Jewish Graceland Cemetery, 30-32
Jewish Waldheim Cemetery, 112-
  116
Johnson, Jack, 24

K

Kahn, Fazlur Rahman, 29
Kathmann Monument, 164
Katz, Ida Balaban, 115
Kelly, Edward, 67
Kenna, Michael "Hinky Dink", 67
Kennelley, Martin, 67
Kennison, David, 12
Kimball, William, 14-15
Kinzie, John, 13-14
Kirby, George, 140
Klacel, Ladimir, 56-57
Knights of Pythias, 100
Kolbe, St. Maximillian, 73
Kolloway, Donald M. Sr., 169
Kolze, Henry, 86
Kozlowski, Anthony, 83
Krupa, Gene, 189, 191
Kupcinet, Karyn "Cookie", 70

L

Latvian cemeteries/sections
Mount Olive, 95
Lawrence Kelly, 65
Lawson, Victor, 21-22
ledgers, 52, 72, 176
Lidice Memorial, the, 57
Lincoln, Abraham, 44
Lincoln Cemetery, 169-172
Lithuanian cemeteries/sections
Lithuanian National, 165-166
St. Casimir, 159
Lithuanian National Cemetery,
165-166
Lombardo, Antonio "The Scourge",
133
Luckman, Sid, 70
Luehring, Emma, 86
Luxembourger cemeteries/sections
St. Henry, 49-52
Lyons, Josie, 68

M

Macedonian cemeteries/sections
Elmwood, 101
Maennerchor, The, 35
Maghett, Samuel G./Magic Sam,
175
Maher, George W., 38
Majestic Radio Corporation, 110
Mantellate Sisters, 179
Mason, Roswell, 45
Masonic cemeteries/sections
Acacia Park, 91-93
Masonic Cemetery, 201
Mount Emblem, 121
Oak Ridge, 124
Masonic Cemetery, 201
Mason's Rest monument, 124

mausoleums
community, 39, 40, 42, 43,
50-52, 70, 91-93, 95, 137,
163, 173
garden, 177
private, 11, 19-21, 25, 26, 32, 35,
36, 55-56, 66, 72, 106, 110,
111, 114-115, 119, 125-126,
130,156, 174, 190
May Chapel, 47
May, John, 133
Mayer, Oscar, 45
Mayslake, 197-198
McCormick, Colonel Robert R., 198
McCormick, Cyrus, 22-23
McGurn, "Machine Gun Jack",
132-133, 135-136
Medill, Joseph, 24
Meisenberg, Samuel, 116
Memorial Park Cemetery, 70
Mexican cemeteries/sections
Montrose, 52
St. Mary, 168
Meyer Family, the, 32
Mies van der Rohe, Ludwig, 27
military monuments
Civil War, 47, 57-58, 60, 63, 65,
149, 174
Spanish-American War, 59, 60
WW I, 49, 73
WW II, 49, 60
Miller, Darius, 38
Milliken, Isaac Lawrence, 45
Moholy-Nagy, László, 27
Monastery of the Most Holy Mother
of God, 202
Montrose Cemetery, 51-52
Moran, "Bugs", 129, 136
Morgan, Helen, 177
Morton, Samuel "Nails", 116
Mount Auburn Cemetery, 120
Mount B'nai B'rith Cemetery, 95
Mount Carmel Cemetery, 125-133

Mount Emblem Cemetery, 121
Mount Glenwood Cemetery, 188-189
Mount Greenwood Cemetery, 157
Mount Hope Cemetery, 174-175
Mount Isaiah Cemetery, 95
Mount Olive Cemetery, 94-95
Mount Olivet Cemetery, 154-156
Mount Mayriv Cemetery, 95
Muhammad, Elijah, 189
Muno, Henry, 49

N

Native American burial grounds
  Robinson Woods, 88
Nelson, "Baby Face", 99
Nickel, Richard, 27
Nitti, Frank "The Enforcer", 133, 135

O

Oak Hill Cemetery, 173
Oak Ridge Cemetery, 123-124
Oak Woods Cemetery, 147-153
Oakland Cemetery, 202
O'Banion, Dion "Deanie", 127-129, 132
Odd Fellows, 109
O'Hare International Airport, 85-86
O'Leary, Catherine, 155-156
Ostrowski, John, 163
Our Lady of Angels Memorial, 137
Owens, Jesse, 152-153

P

Palestinian cemeteries/sections
  Evergreen, 167
Palmer, Bertha Honoré, 19-20

Palmer, Potter, 19-20
Palmer, Walter, 77
Parsons, Lucy, 105
Peabody, Francis Stuyvesant, 197
Pearce, Frances, 48
Pedrini, Reverend Mother Louis, 179
Perkins, Dwight, 28
Pershing, John J. (parents of), 147
pet cemeteries, 121, 141
Peter II, 202
Petta, Julia Buccola, 126-127
"Phantom General", 47
Piccolo, Brian, 168
Pinkerton, Allan, 23
Polish cemeteries/sections
  All Saints Polish National Catholic, 83
  Holy Cross, 189-191
  Resurrection, 163-164
  St. Adalbert, 71-74
Poole, Robert, *see* Muhammed, Elijah
Protestant cemeteries
  All Saints Polish National Catholic, 83
  Altenheim, 120
  Bethania, 164
  Bohemian National, 53-63
  Church of the Holy Comforter, 69
  Concordia, 118-119
  Forest Home/German Waldheim, 102-111
  Lithuanian National, 165-166
  St. John's/St. Johannes, 85-86
  Wunder's, 33
Puerto Rican cemeteries/sections
  Montrose, 52
Pullman, George, 15

Q

Queen of Heaven Cemetery, 134-140
Quinn, Mary Alice, 176-177

R

Ransom, Major General Thomas E.G., 47
Rayne, Martha Louise, 109
Reed, Jimmy, 169-170
Reed, Robert, 70
Rest Haven Cemetery, 85-86
Restvale Cemetery, 175
Resurrection Cemetery, 163-164
Ricca, Paul "The Waiter", 134-135
Rice, John Blake, 45
Ridgelawn Cemetery, 62
Robinson Family, the, 88
Robinson Woods Indian Burial Ground, 88
Roche, John, 45
Roebuck, Alvah, 91-92
Root, John Wellborn, 29
Root, Joseph Cullen, 122
Rosehill Cemetery, 37-48
Rosemont Park Cemetery, 95
Rosenwald, Julius, 38
Ross, David Barney, 95
Rotary International Memorial, 174
Ruby, Jack, 90
Ruekheim, Robert, 49
Russian cemeteries/sections
    Elmwood, 101
Ryerson, Martin, 25

S

Sabath, Adolph J., 110
St. Adalbert Cemetery, 71-74

St. Benedict Cemetery, 179
St. Boniface Cemetery, 34-36
St. Casimir, 159
St. Henry Cemetery, 49-52
St. James-Sag Cemetery, 184-187
St. John/St. Johannes Cemetery, 85-86
St. Joseph Cemetery, 99-100
St. Mary, 168
St. Nicholas Ukrainian Cemetery, 84
St. Sava Orthodox Monastery, 202
Saint Valentine's Day Massacre, 94, 132-133
Salerno, Francesco, 131
Saperstein, Abe, 89
sarcophagi, 18, 30, 50, 84
Scandinavian cemeteries/sections
    Elmwood, 101
    Mount Olive, 94-95
    Oak Hill, 173
Schalk, Ray, 167
Schmidt, Lars, 107
Schmidt, Ruth, 107
Schmitt George, 38
Schoenhofen, Peter, 20
Schwimmer, Reinhart, 45
Schwinn, Ignaz, 37-38
Scott, Robert S., 38
Sears, Richard Warren, 38, 42
Serbian cemeteries/sections
    Monastery of the Most Holy Mother of God, 202
    Montrose, 52
    St. Sava Orthodox Monastery, 202
Shalom Memorial Park, 78
Shedd, John G., 42-43
Showmen's Rest, 117-118
Shrine of the Holy Innocents, 137
Siefert, August, 69
Siskel, Gene, 90
Skinner, James Fletcher, 111

Smyth, John M., 67
Snyder, James L., 169
Soldiers' Home, 149
Spanish-American War monuments,
   59, 60
Spann, Otis, 179
Spinner, Phillipp, 69
Starrett, Vincent, 23
Stephen A. Douglas Memorial Park,
   195
Stejskal-Buchal Family, the, 55
Strasser, Adolph, 109
Stroud, Robert, 201-202
Sunday, Bill, 109, 111
Sunset Memorial Park, 76
Sullivan, Louis, 27
Swift, George Bell, 45
Swift, Gustavus, 174

T

Thompson, William Hale, 148-149
Todd, Michael, 109
Torrio, John, 127-129
Touhy, Roger, 133
Tower of Remembrance, 78

U

Ukrainian cemeteries/sections
   Elmwood, 101
   Evergreen Cemetery, 167
   St. Nicholas Ukrainian, 83
United Ancient Order of Druids,
   108-109
United Spanish War Veterans
   Memorial, 60

V

Volk, Leonard, 39
Volunteer Fireman's Monument, 39

W

Wacker, Charles, 20-21
Wajciechowski, Earl, *see* Weiss,
   "Hymie"
Walsh, Artie, 66-67
Walsh, Willie, 66-67
Ward, Aaron Montgomery, 38, 42
Warsaw Benevolent Association
   Cemetery, 115
Washington, Dinah, 178
Washington, Harold, 146-147, 149
Waters, Muddy, 175
Weaver, George D. "Buck", 174
Webster, Timothy, 24
Weinshank, Albert, 116
Weiss, "Hymie", 116, 132, 136
Wells, Ida B., 149
Welsh cemeteries/sections
   Forest Home/German Waldheim,
      103
Wentworth, Mayor "Long John", 43
Westlawn Cemetery, 89-90
Westphal, Adolph, 111
Wightkin,William, 140
Willard, Frances, 39
Wolff, Albert N. "Wallpaper", 90
Woodlawn Cemetery, 117-118
World War I monuments, 49, 60, 73
World War II monuments, 49, 60
Wrigley Field, 198-199
Wunder's Cemetery, 33

Y

Yorktown Shopping Center, 195

Z

Zoroastrian cemeteries/sections
   Elm Lawn, 121

ABOUT THE AUTHORS

Ursula Bielski grew up in a haunted house on Chicago's north side. At an early age she became a believer in paranormal experiences, from the curse of the Chicago Cubs at nearby Wrigley Field to the hauntings at local Graceland Cemetery by a 19th century ghost girl. Underscoring these neighborhood folktales were accounts by her police officer father of personal encounters with Big Foot and no less than the Devil himself.

Bielski holds an M.A. in American intellectual and cultural history. Her academic explorations include the spiritualist movement of the 19th century and its transformation into psychical research and parapsychology, and the relationship between belief and experience, science and religion. These interests led her to join investigations of reported hauntings of such notorious sites as the Country House Restaurant in suburban Clarendon Hills; Chicago's Red Lion Pub; and the Oshkosh, Wisconsin Opera House.

Intrigued by the apparent relationship between folklore and paranormal experience, Bielski eventually turned her interests toward her hometown, penning her acclaimed and widely successful book, *Chicago Haunts: Ghostlore of the Windy City*. After several printings of the book and the release of a second edition, Bielski now lectures regularly on the subject.

Bielski is editor of *PA News*, the quarterly bulletin of the Parapsychology Association. She is currently at work on a

children's cookbook inspired by the gothic novels of John
Bellairs as well as a second volume of *Chicago Haunts*. She lives
in Chicago with her husband, author David Cowan, and their
daughter.

Matt Hucke is a
UNIX programmer
and Internet consul-
tant living in the
Rogers Park neigh-
borhood of Chicago.
He has been explor-
ing, photographing,
and writing about
Chicago cemeteries
since 1995. His im-
ages of graveyards have appeared in both editions of *Chicago
Haunts: Ghostlore of the Windy City*, the *American Girls News*,
and the *Washington Post*, and have been used online by the
Chicago Historical Society and the *San Diego Union-Tribune*.

In 1996 Hucke created the Web site that inspired this book,
"Graveyards of Chicago," which can be found at *http://www.
graveyards.com*. The site has since grown to include over 600
photographs.

Matt's favorite Chicago graveyard is Rosehill.

PUBLISHER'S CREDITS

Cover Design by Timothy Kocher.

Photos by Matt Hucke.

Editing by Bruce Clorfene.

Interior Design and Layout by Sharon Woodhouse.

Proofreading by Sharon Woodhouse, Susan McNulty, and Brandon Zamora.

Indexing by Brandon Zamora and Sharon Woodhouse.

Back Cover Text by David Cowan

The text of *Graveyards of Chicago* was set in the Hearse font.

NOTE

Although Lake Claremont Press, the authors, editor, and others affiliated with *Graveyards of Chicago* have exhaustively researched all sources to ensure the accuracy and completeness of the information contained within this book, we assume no responsibility for errors, inaccuracies, omissions, or inconsistency herein. Special care was taken to preserve respect for the deceased and any slights of people or organizations are unintentional.

LAKE CLAREMONT PRESS FAVORITES

Chicago Haunts: Ghostlore of the Windy City
(Revised Edition)
by Ursula Bielski
From ruthless gangsters to restless mail order kings, from the Fort Dearborn Massacre to the St. Valentine's Day Massacre, the phantom remains of the passionate people and volatile events of Chicago history have made the Second City second to none in the annals of American ghostlore. Bielski captures over 160 years of this haunted history with her unique blend of lively storytelling, in-depth historical research, exclusive interviews, and insights from parapsychology. Called "a masterpiece of the genre," "a must-read," and "an absolutely first-rate-book" by reviewers, *Chicago Haunts* continues to earn the praise of critics and readers alike.
0-9642426-7-2, October 1998, softcover, 277 pages, 29 photos, $15

Hollywood on Lake Michigan:
100 Years of Chicago and the Movies
by Arnie Bernstein
This engaging history and street guide finally gives Chicago and Chicagoans due credit for their prominent role in moviemaking history, from the silent era to the present. With trivia, special articles, historic and contemporary photos, film profiles, anecdotes, and exclusive interviews with dozens of personalities, including Studs Terkel, Roger Ebert, Gene Siskel, Dennis Franz, Harold Ramis, Joe Mantegna, Bill Kurtis, Irma Hall, and Tim Kazurinsky. Foreword by *Soul Food* writer/director, George Tillman, Jr.
0-9642426-2-1, December 1998, softcover, 364 pages, 80 photos, $15

Know More, Spend Less:
A Native's Guide To Chicago, 3rd Edition
by Sharon Woodhouse,
With expanded South Side coverage by Mary McNulty
Venture into the nooks and crannies of everyday Chicago with this unique, comprehensive budget guide. Over 400 pages of free, inexpensive, and unusual things to do in the Windy City make this the perfect resource for tourists, business travelers, visiting suburbanites, and resident Chicagoans. Called the "best guidebook for locals" in *New City* newspaper's 1999 "Best of Chicago" issue!
0-9642426-0-5, January 1999, softcover, 438 pages, photos, maps, $12.95

Whether you're a life-long resident, new in town, or just passing through, let the *Native's Guide* series for Chicago's suburban regions be your personal tour guides of the best our suburbs have to offer.

A Native's Guide to Chicago's Northern Suburbs
by Jason Fargo
0-9642426-8-0, June 1999, softcover, 207 pages, photos, maps, $12.95

A Native's Guide to Chicago's Northwest Suburbs
by Martin A. Bartels
1-893121-00-3, August 1999, softcover, 315 pages, photos, maps, $12.95

A Native's Guide to Chicago's Western Suburbs
by Laura Mazzuca Toops and John W. Toops, Jr.
0-9642426-6-4, August 1999, softcover, 210 pages, photos, maps, $12.95

A Native's Guide to Chicago's South Suburbs
by Christina Bultinck and Christy Johnston-Czarnecki
0-9642426-1-3, June 1999, softcover, 242 pages, photos, maps, $12.95

Full of the fascinating sights, places, stories, and facts that sometimes even locals don't know about, the *Native's Guide* series equips you with everything you need to enjoy and navigate Chicago and its suburbs like a true insider.

ORDER FORM

Please send me autographed copies of the following
Lake Claremont Press titles:

Graveyards of Chicago	_____ @ $15.00 =	_____
Chicago Haunts	_____ @ $15.00 =	_____
Hollywood on Lake Michigan:	_____ @ $15.00 =	_____
A Native's Guide to Chicago, 3rd Ed.	_____ @ $12.95 =	_____
...Guide To Chicago's Northern Suburbs	_____ @ $12.95 =	_____
...Guide To Chicago's Northwest Suburbs	_____ @ $12.95 =	_____
...Guide To Chicago's Western Suburbs	_____ @ $12.95 =	_____
...Guide To Chicago's South Suburbs	_____ @ $12.95 =	_____

Discounts when you order multiple copies!

2 books—10% off total
3-4 books —20% off total
5-9 books—25% off total
10+ books—40% off total

Subtotal: _____

Less Discount: _____

New Subtotal: _____

8.75% tax for
Illinois Residents: _____

Shipping Fees

$2 for the first book and
$.50 for each additional
book or a maximum of $5.

Shipping: _____

TOTAL: _____

Name_____

Address_____

City_____State_____Zip_____

Please enclose check, money order, or credit card number.

Visa/Mastercard#_____Exp. _____

Signature_____

Lake Claremont Press
P.O. Box 25291
Chicago, IL 60625
773/784-7517, 773/784-6504 (fx)
order@lakeclaremont.com

Order by mail, phone, fax, or e-mail.
All of our books have a no-hassle, 100%
money back guarantee.

MORE CHICAGO BOOKS FROM LAKE CLAREMONT PRESS

Chicago Haunts: Ghostlore of the Windy City
by Ursula Bielski

Hollywood on Lake Michigan:
100 Years of Chicago and the Movies
by Arnie Bernstein

Know More, Spend Less: A Native's Guide To Chicago, 3rd Edition
by Sharon Woodhouse
with expanded South Side coverage by Mary McNulty

A Native's Guide To Chicago's Northern Suburbs
by Jason Fargo

A Native's Guide to Chicago's Northwest Suburbs
by Martin A. Bartels

A Native's Guide To Chicago's Western Suburbs
by Laura Mazzuca Toops and John W. Toops, Jr.

A Native's Guide To Chicago's South Suburbs
by Christina Bultinck and Christy Johnston-Czarnecki

COMING IN 2000

The Chicago River: A Natural and Unnatural History
by Libby Hill

"The Movies Are": Carl Sandburg's Film Reviews and Essays, 1920-1928
Edited and with historical commentary by Arnie Bernstein

Literary Chicago: A Book Lover's Tour of the Windy City
by Gregory Holden

Chicago Resource Guide for the Chronically Ill and Disabled
by Susan McNulty